This journal belongs to:

_____

We Are A GROWTH MINDSET *family*

Feels like

Sounds like

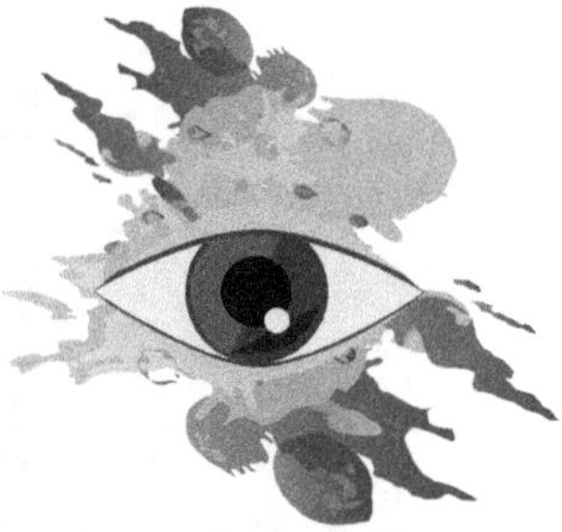

Looks like

THEY LEARN FROM FEEDBACK

THEY LOVE LEARNING

THEY ASK FOR HELP

What happens when someone has a GROWTH MINDSET?

THEY NEVER GIVE UP

THEY KNOW CHANGE TAKES TIME

THEY ARE NOT AFRAID TO FAIL

THEY PUT FORTH EFFORT

THEY GET INSPIRED BY OTHERS

Perseverance

Perseverance is all about not giving up when things get really tough. Write about someone you know who has great perseverance. How does this person show perserverance?

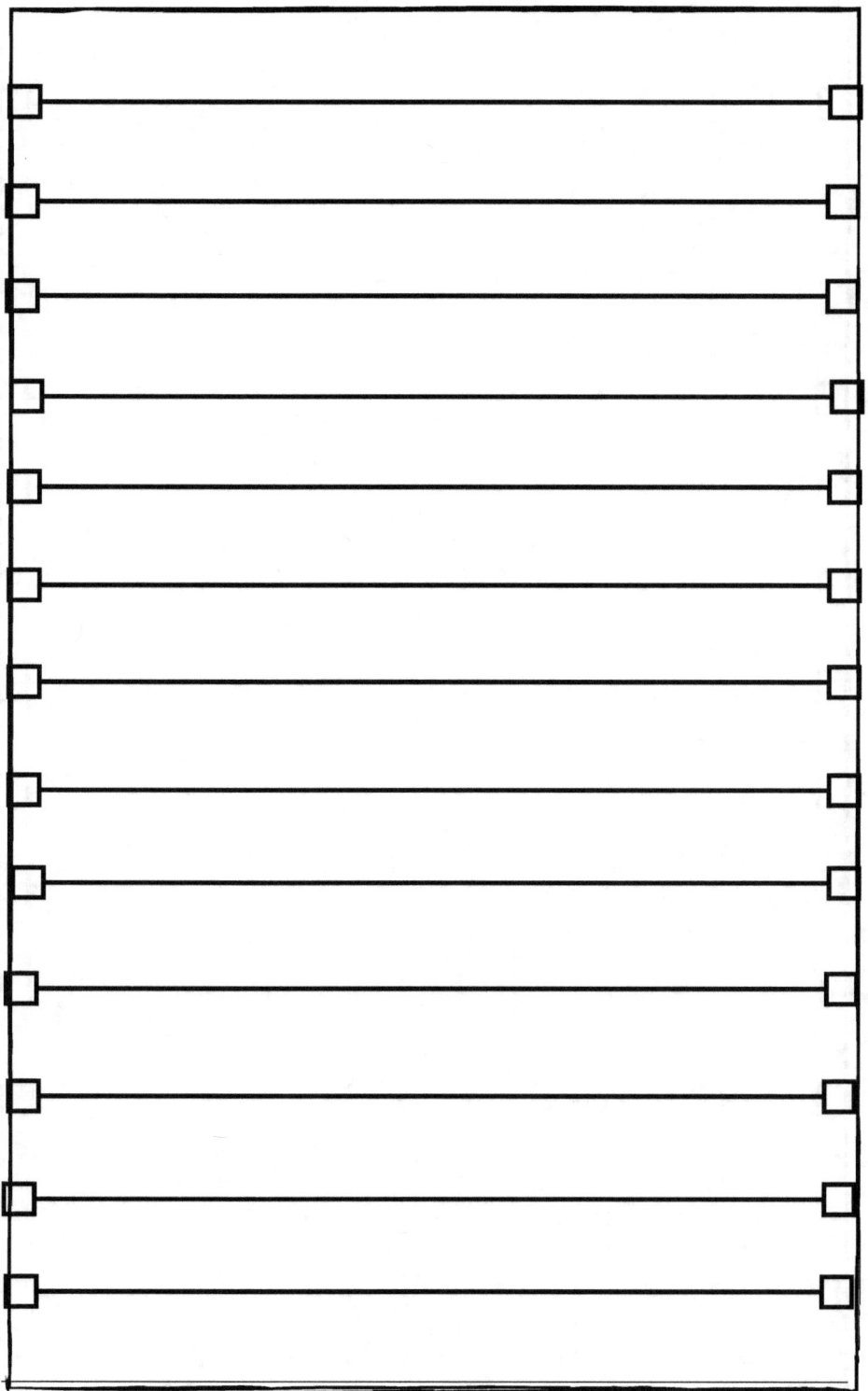

Would you rather?

When you grow up, would you rather have a boring job where you make a lot of money or have a job that makes you happy and challenges you, but make less money? Why?

What challenge did you work out today?

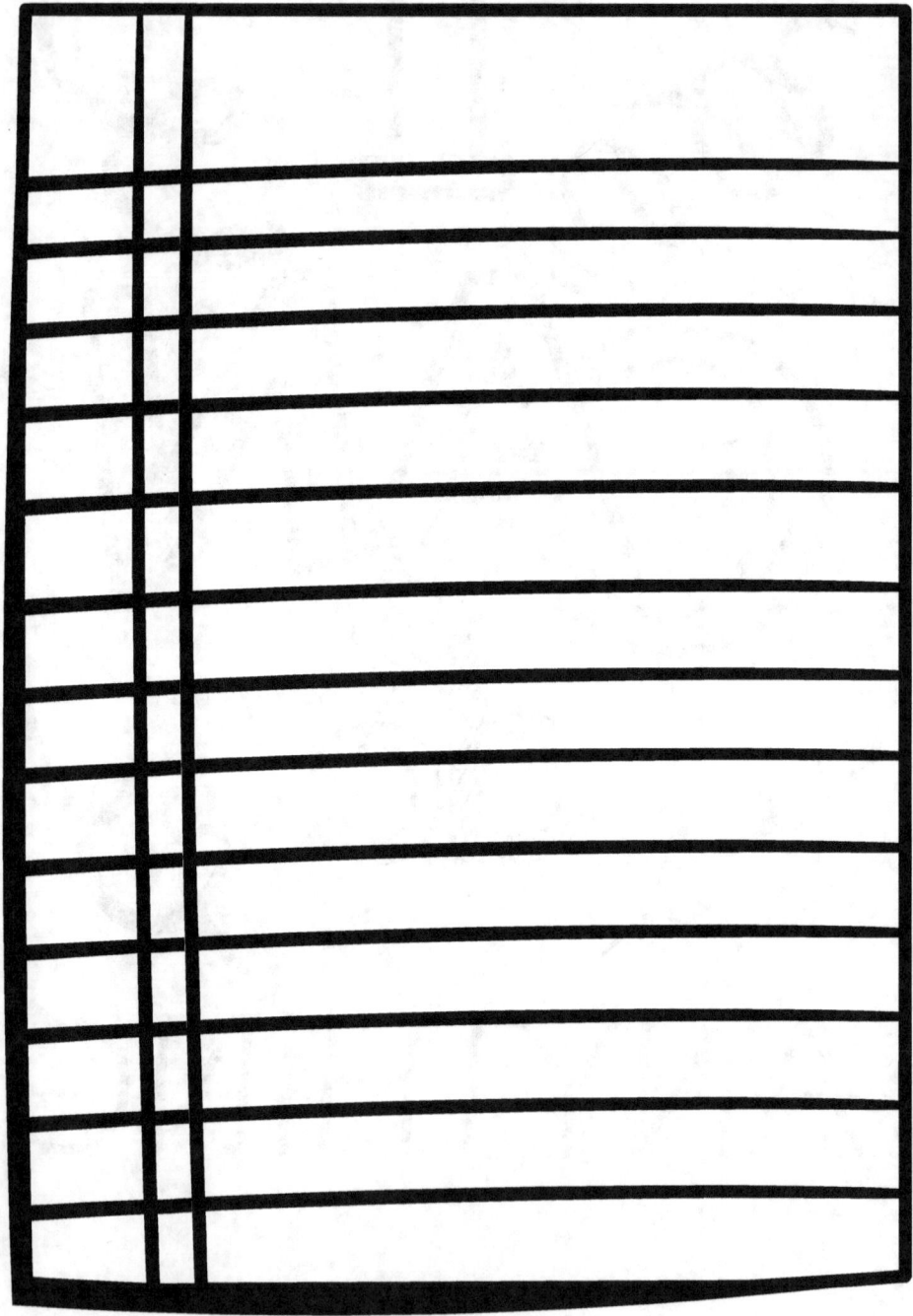

My Goal Think-Sheet

Things I would like to get better at:

_____
_____
_____
_____

I will be proud of myself if I accomplish this:

_____
_____
_____
_____

I would like to do this if I knew I couldn't fail:

_____
_____
_____
_____

Acts of Kindess

Things people did for me:

_____
_____
_____
_____
_____
_____
_____
_____

Things I did for other people:

_____
_____
_____
_____
_____
_____
_____
_____

I AM STRONG
I AM AMAZING
I AM KIND
I AM BEAUTIFUL
I AM HAPPY
I AM BRAVE
I AM SMART

What challenge did you work out today?

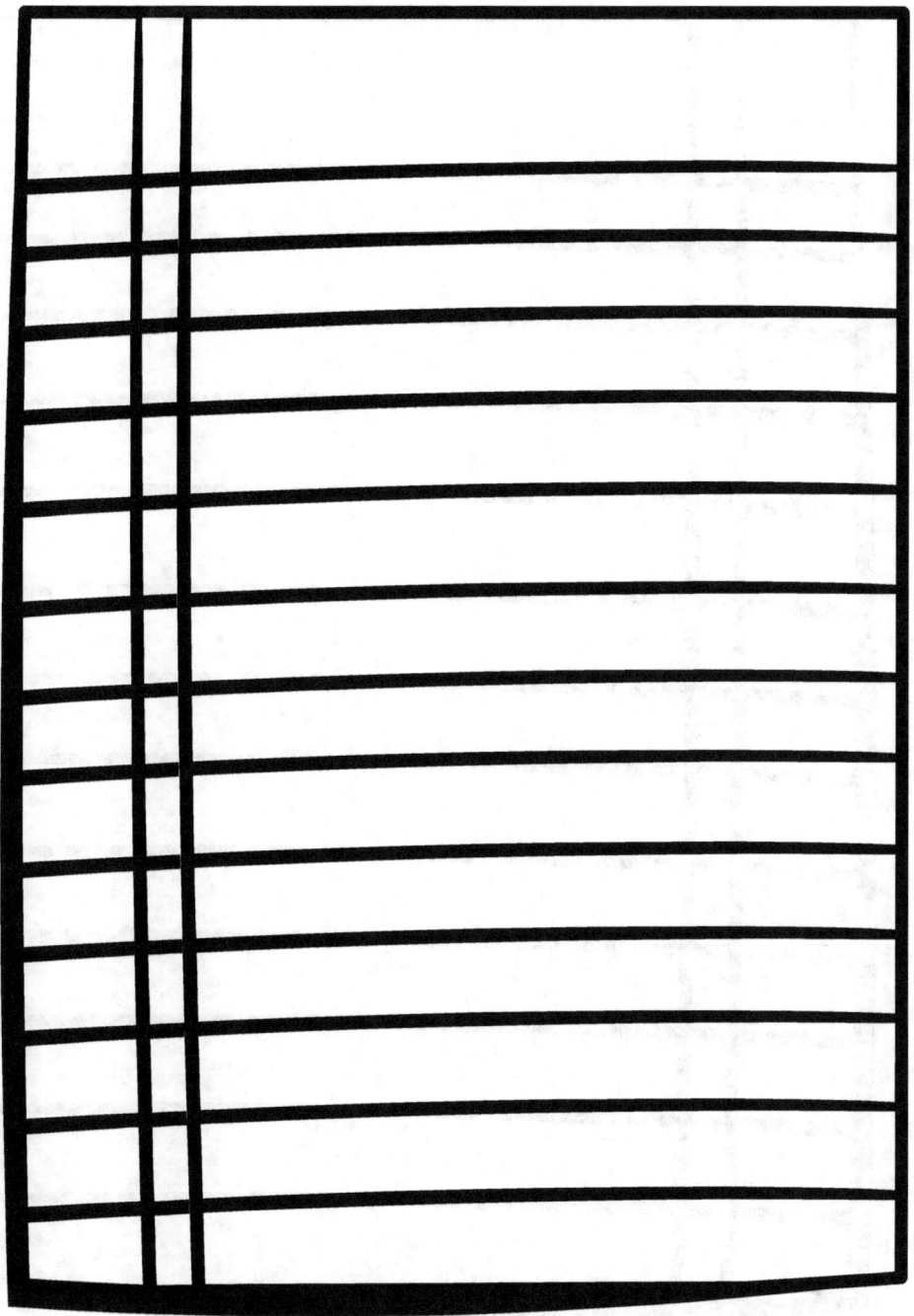

What challenge did you work out today?

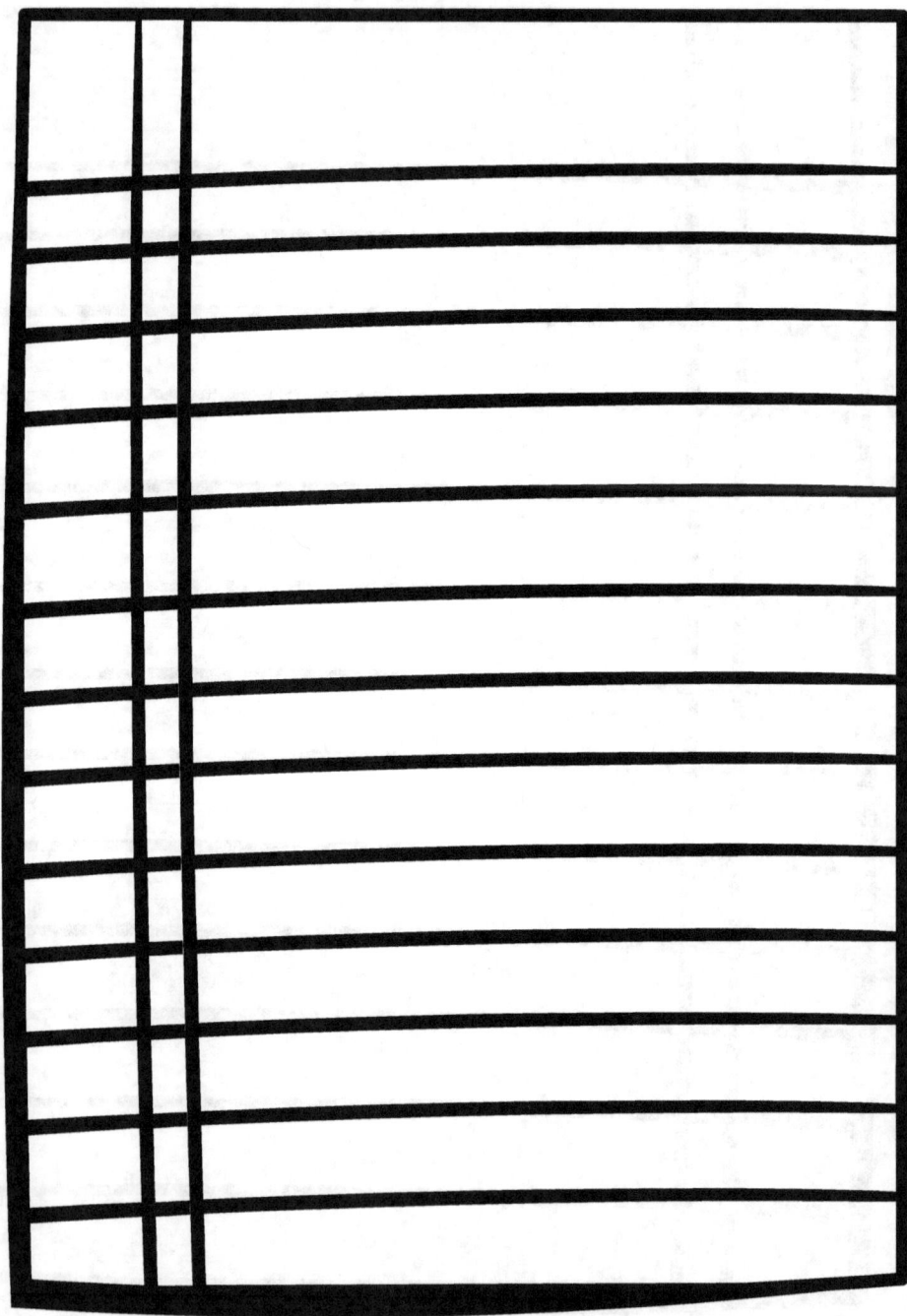

What challenge did you work out today?

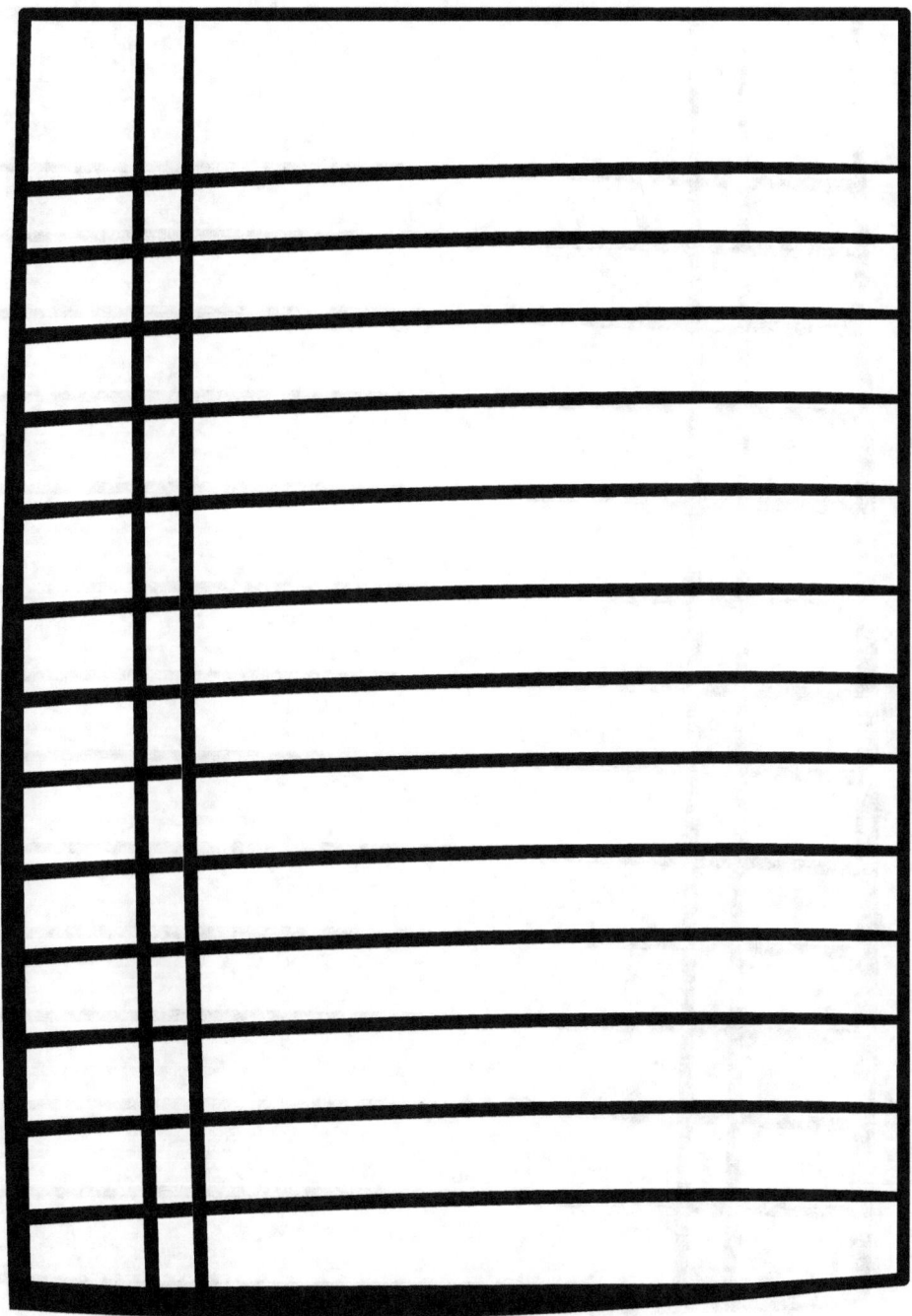

Notes:

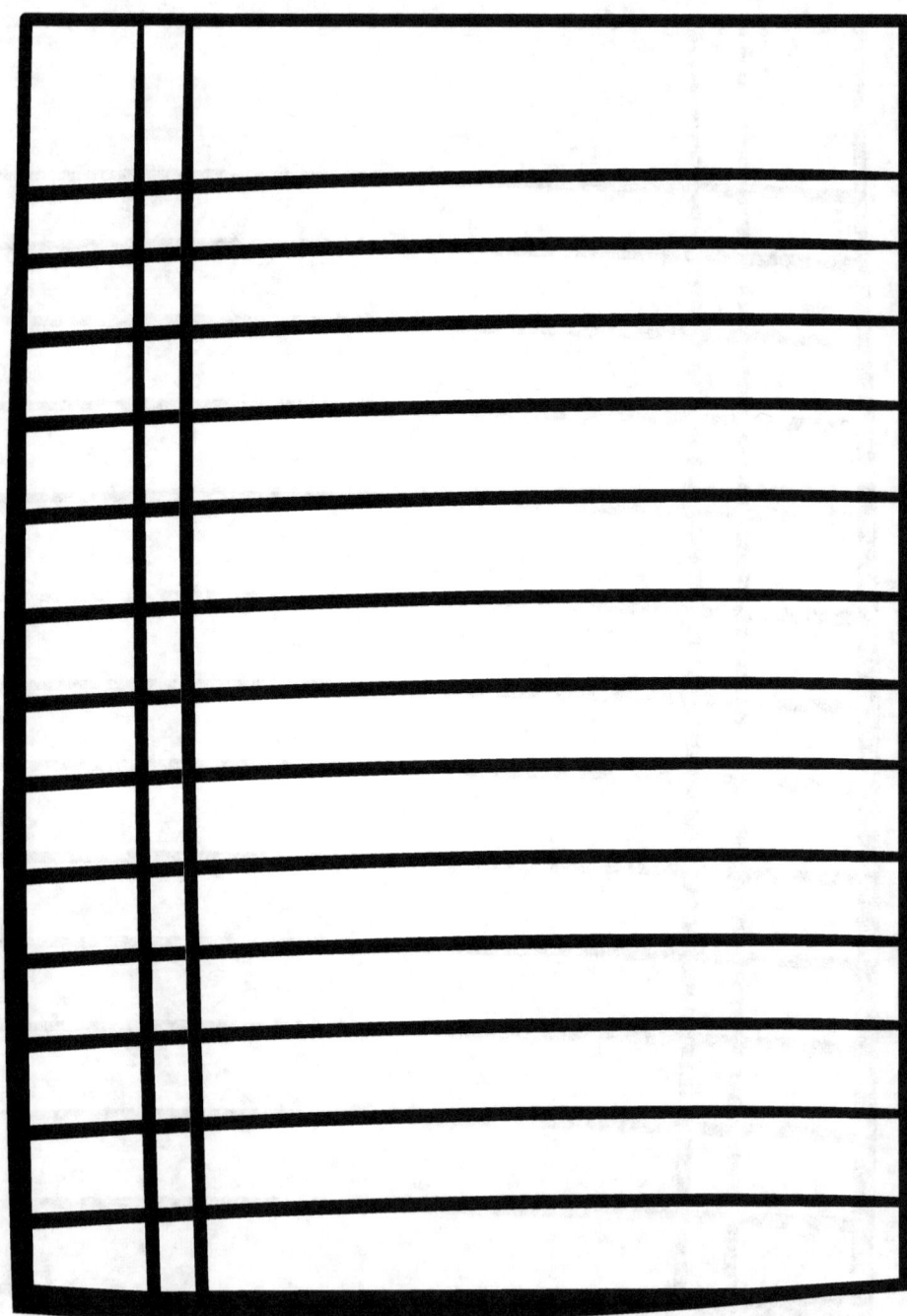

Notes:

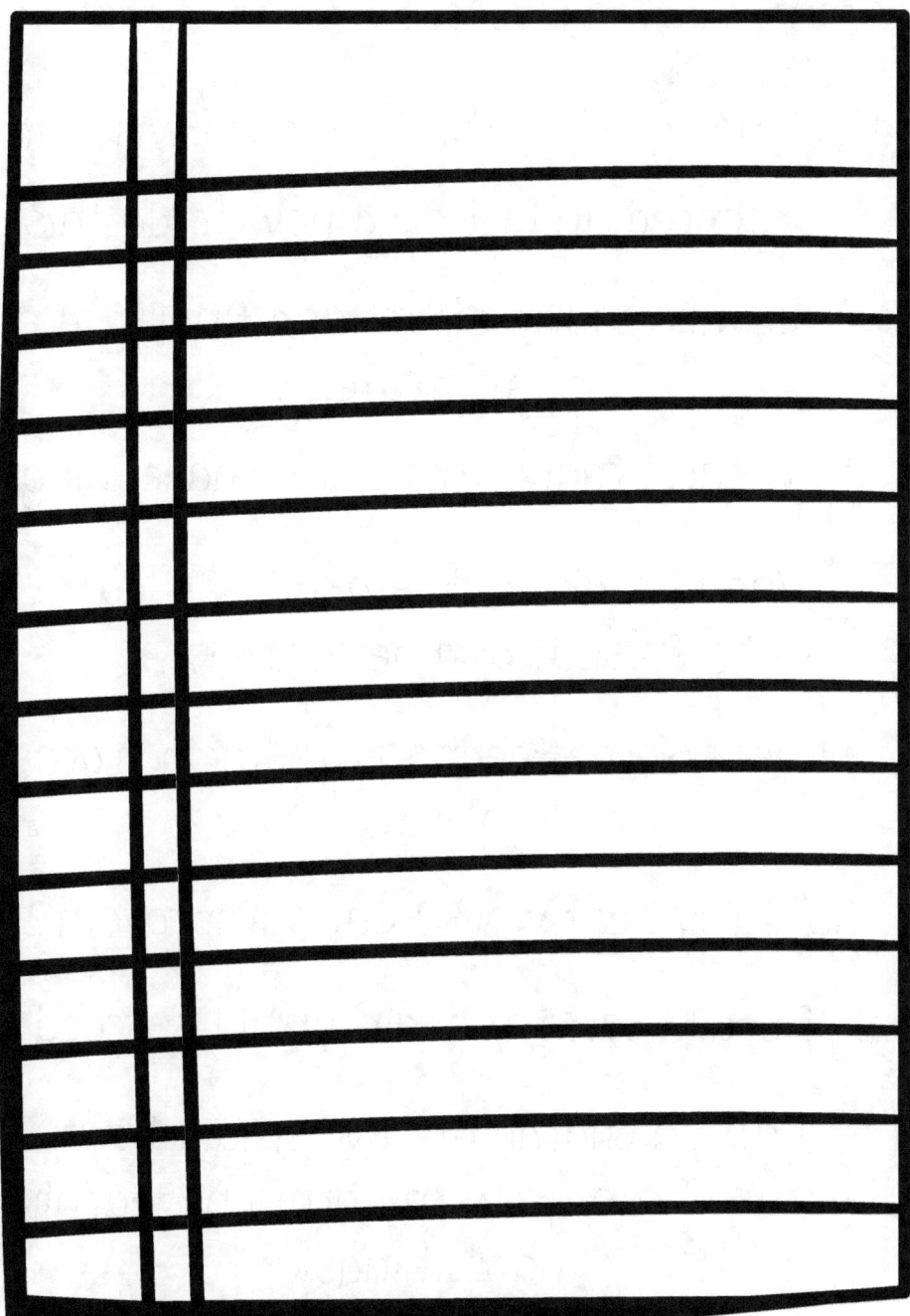

I can CHANGE my MINDSET with my WORDS

I CAN SAY:

I am not good at this YET, but I will learn.

I practiced and learned how to do this.

This will require effort and finding the right strategy.

How can I make this more challenging?

When I make a mistake, I will learn from it and get better.

I need some feedback and help from others.

Is it my best work? Can I improve it?

If I fail I can try again until I succeed.

I am in charge of how smart I am because I can grow my brain by learning hard things!

I can CHANGE my MINDSET with my WORDS

INSTEAD OF:

I am not good at this.

I am great at this.

This is too hard.

This is too easy.

I am afraid I will make a mistake.

I give up.

I can't do this.

This is good enough.

I won't try because I might fail.

I am not as smart as my friend.

What is your favorite way to feel calm?

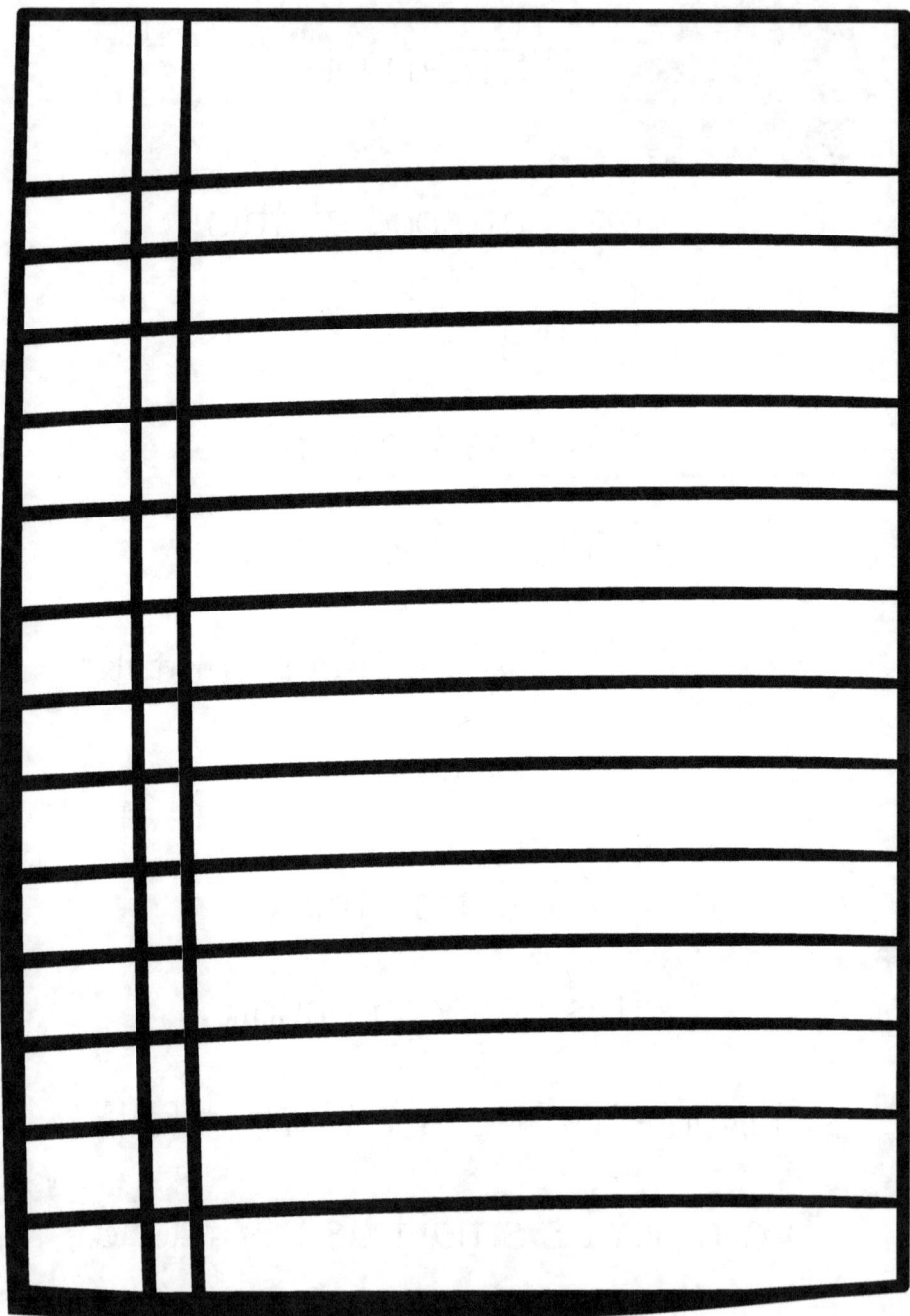

What did you learn today?

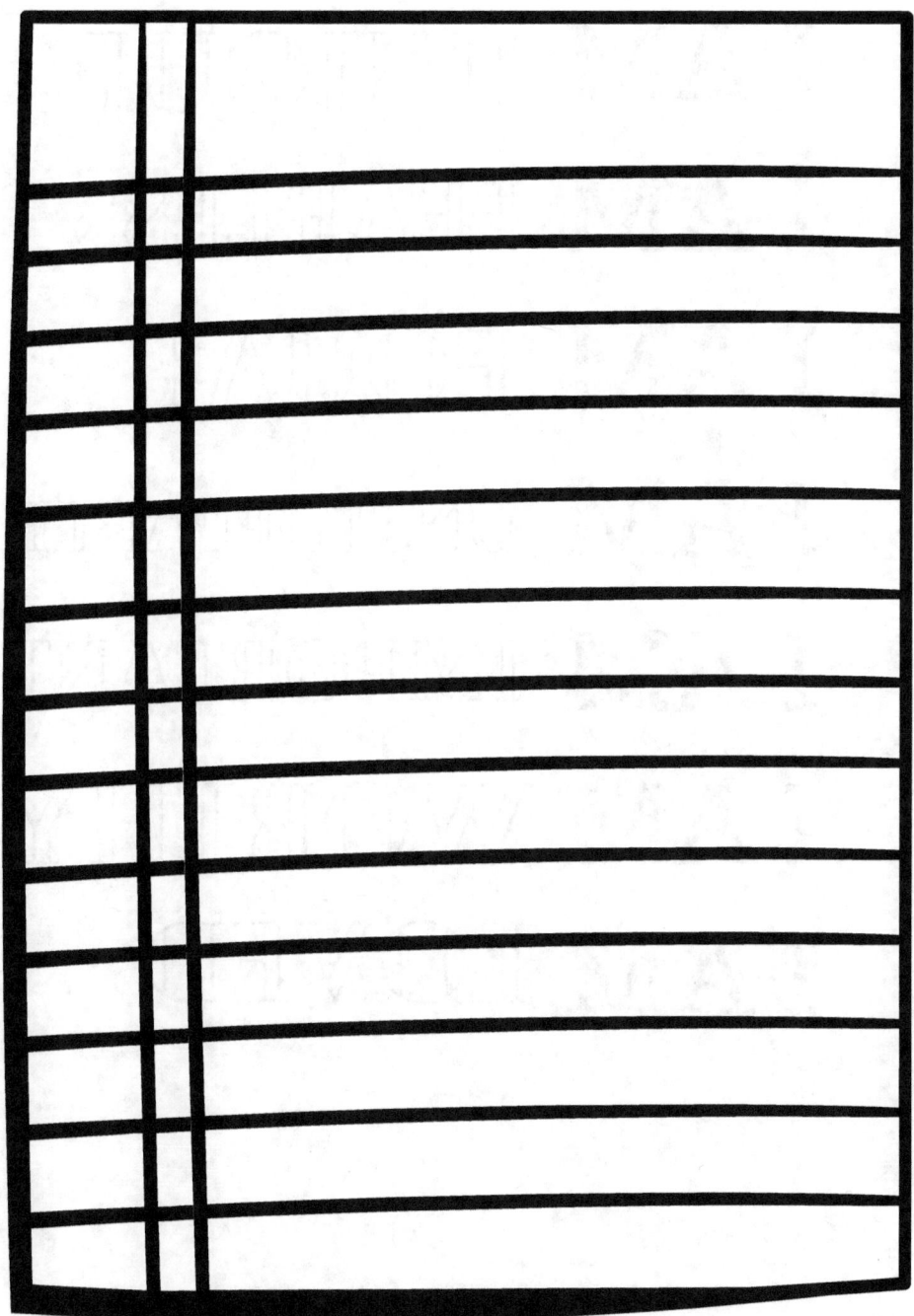

I AM UNIQUE
I AM FEARLESS
I AM EQUAL
I AM UNSTOPPABLE
I AM IMPORTANT
I AM WORTHY
I AM LOVED

Notes:

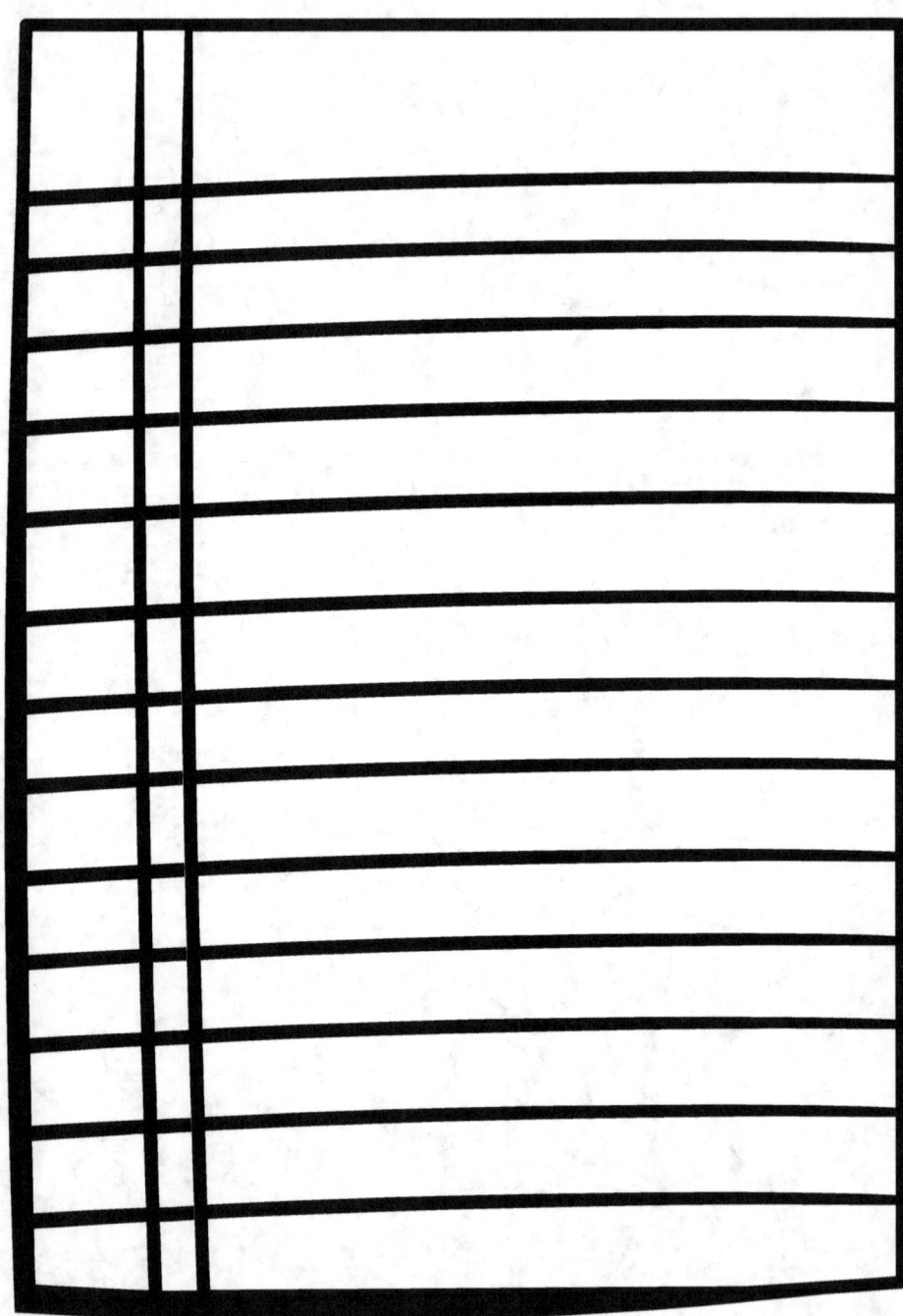

Notes:

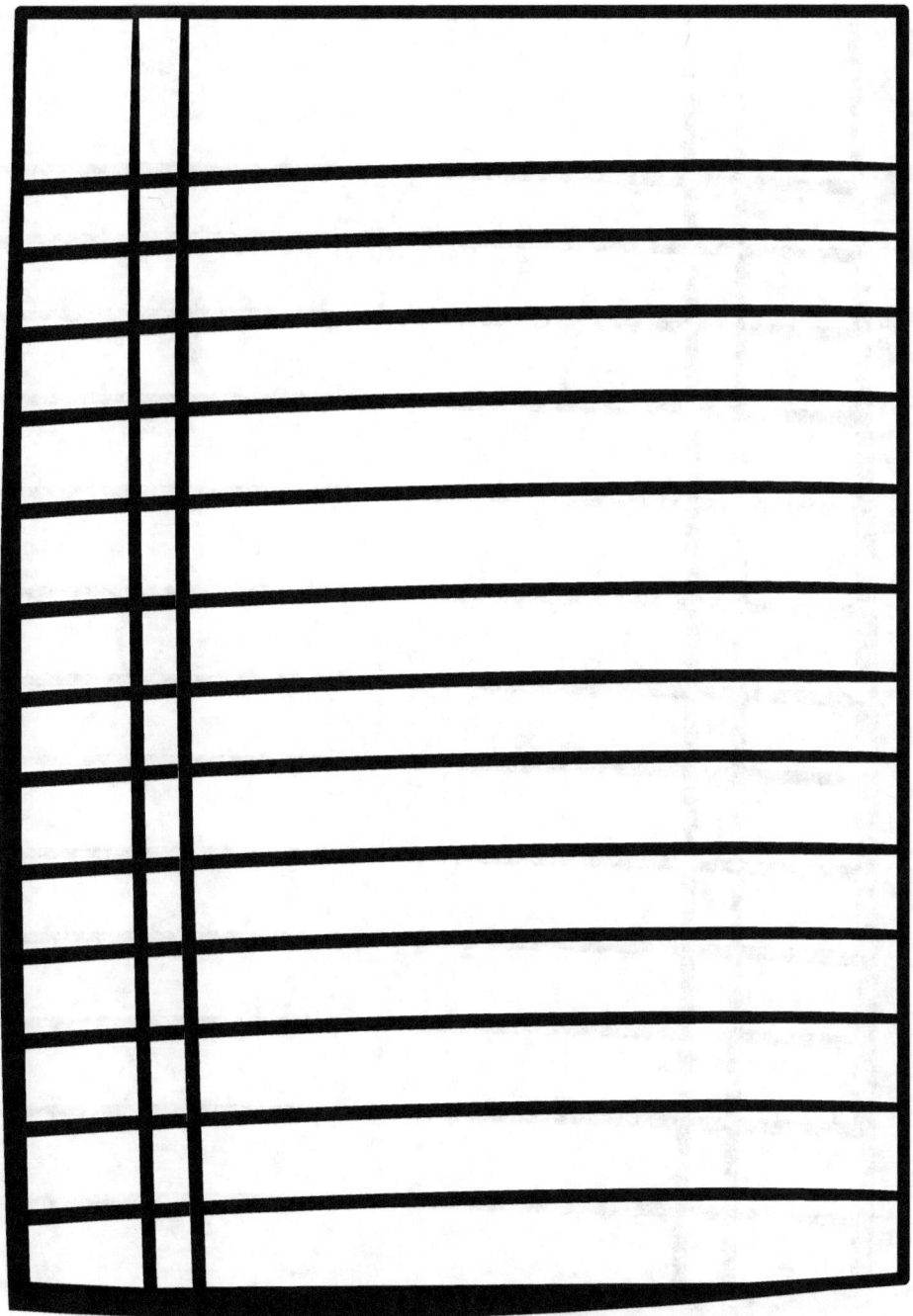

Notes:

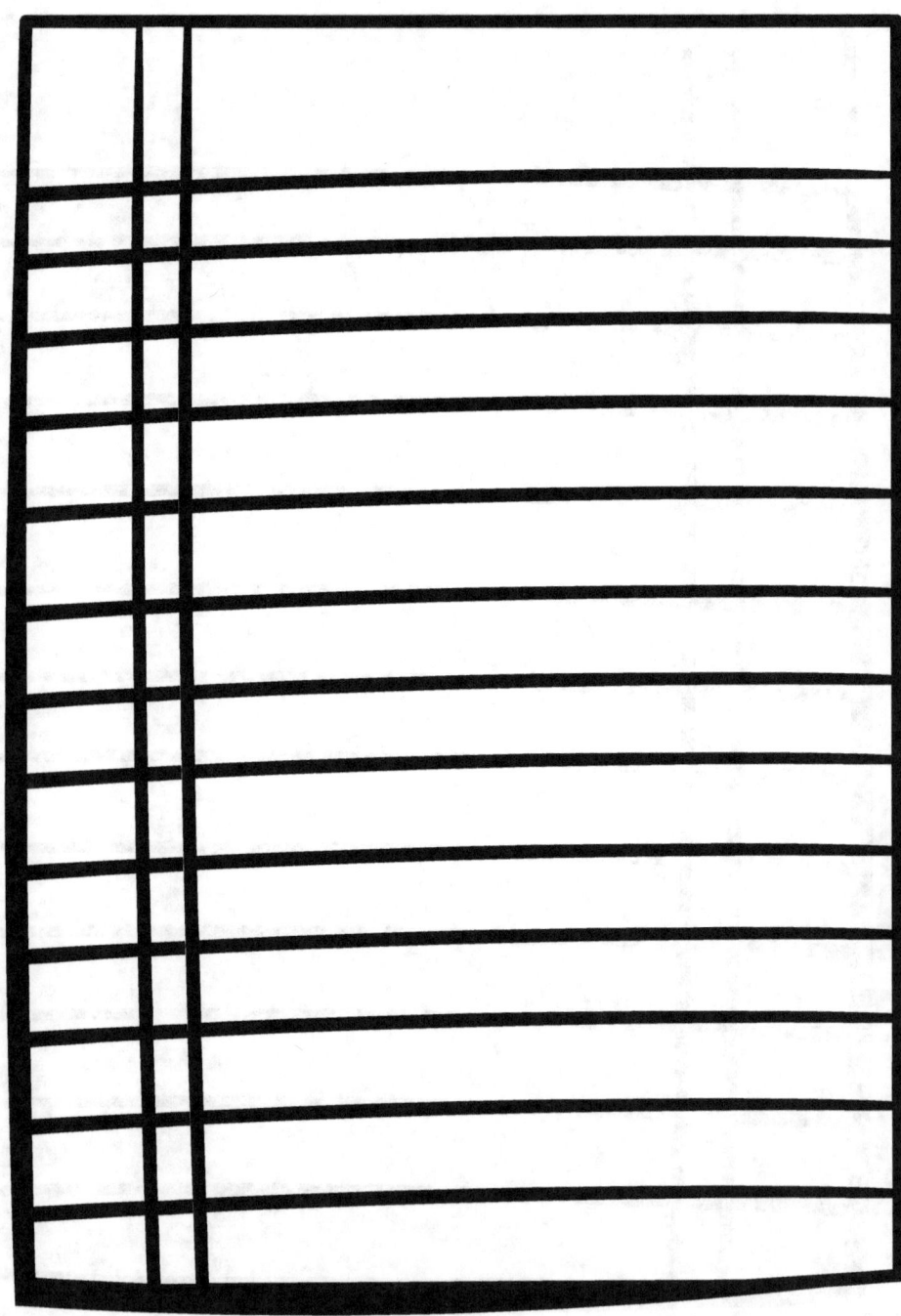

Notes:

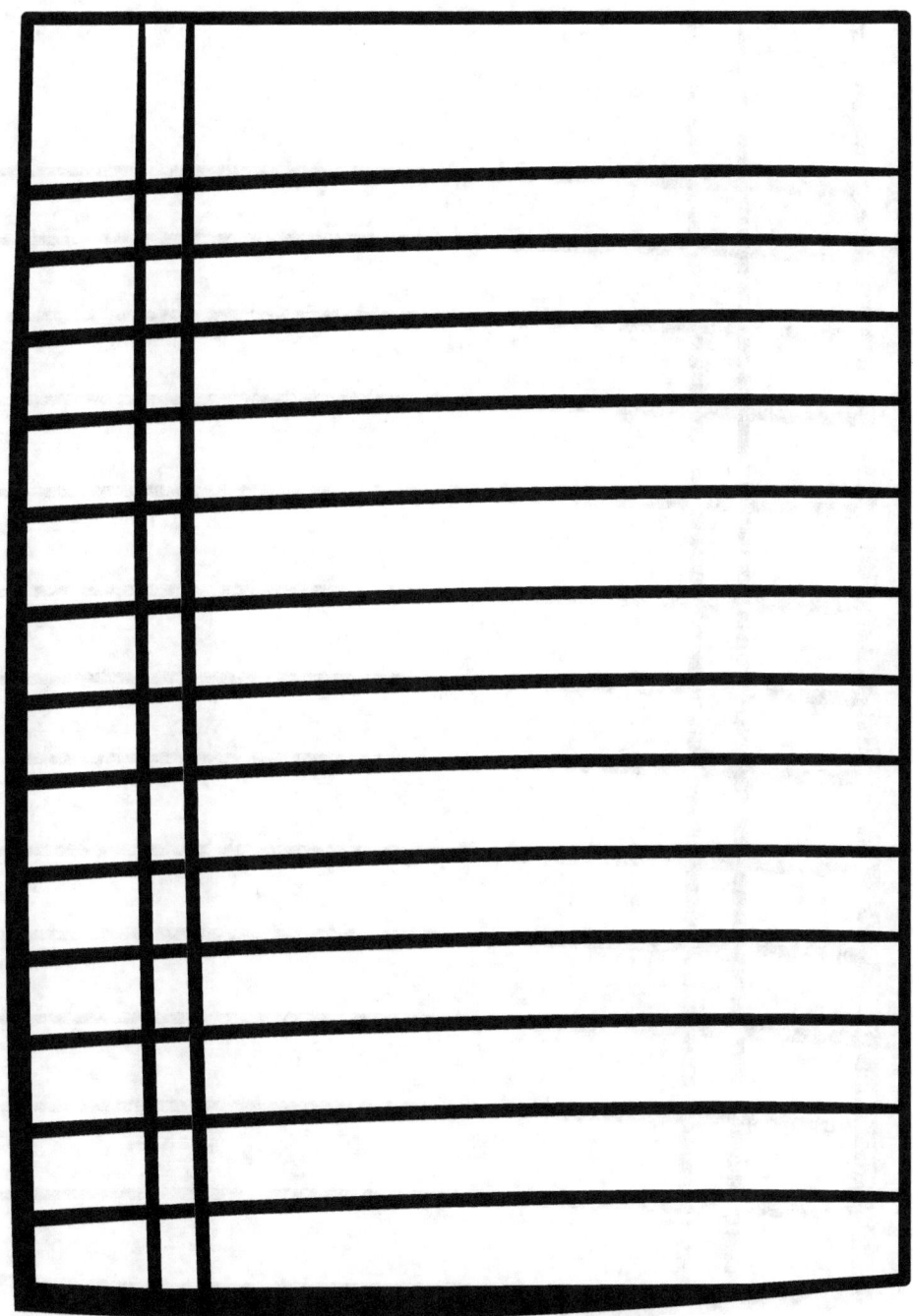

Notes:

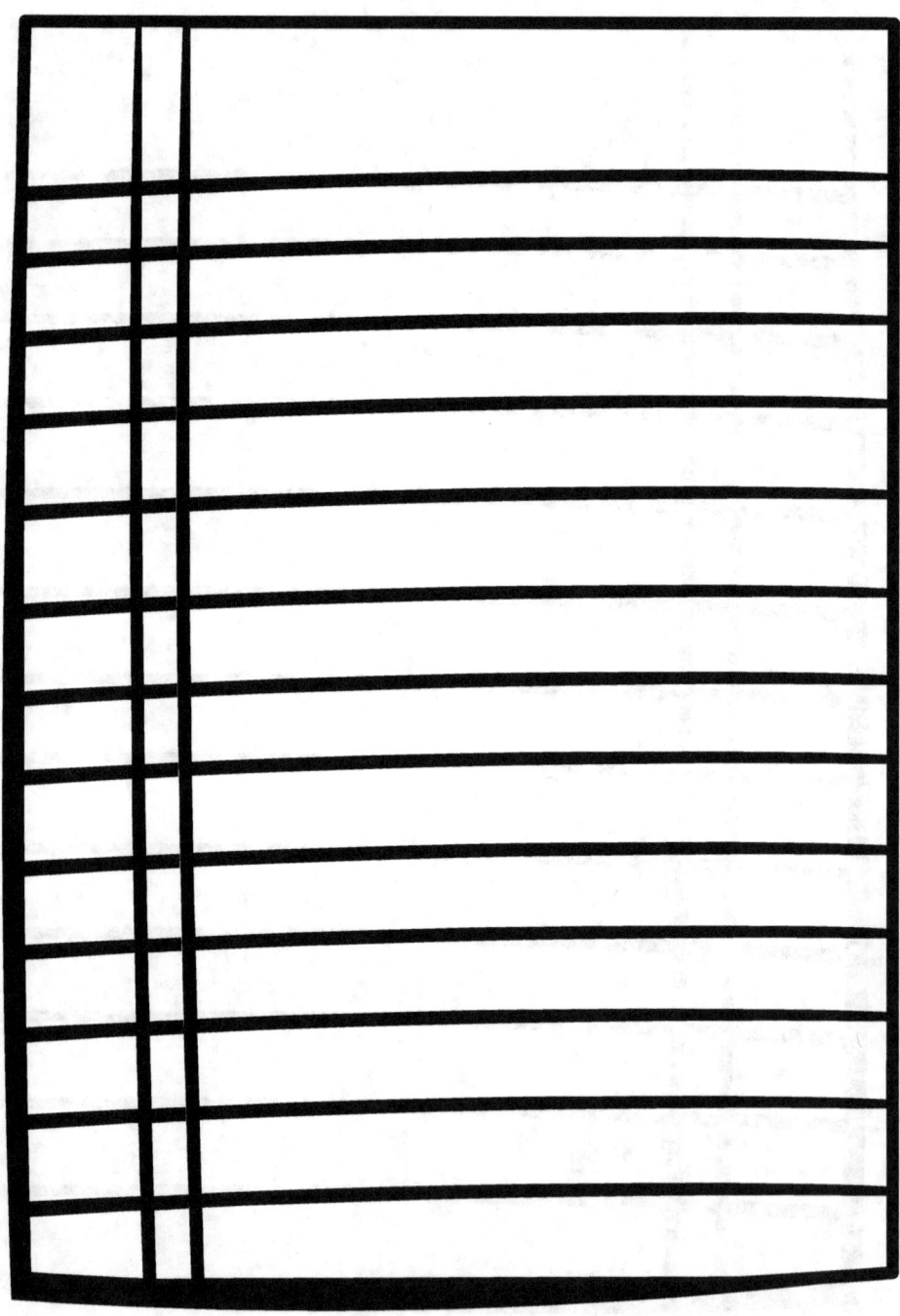

What would you like to get better at?

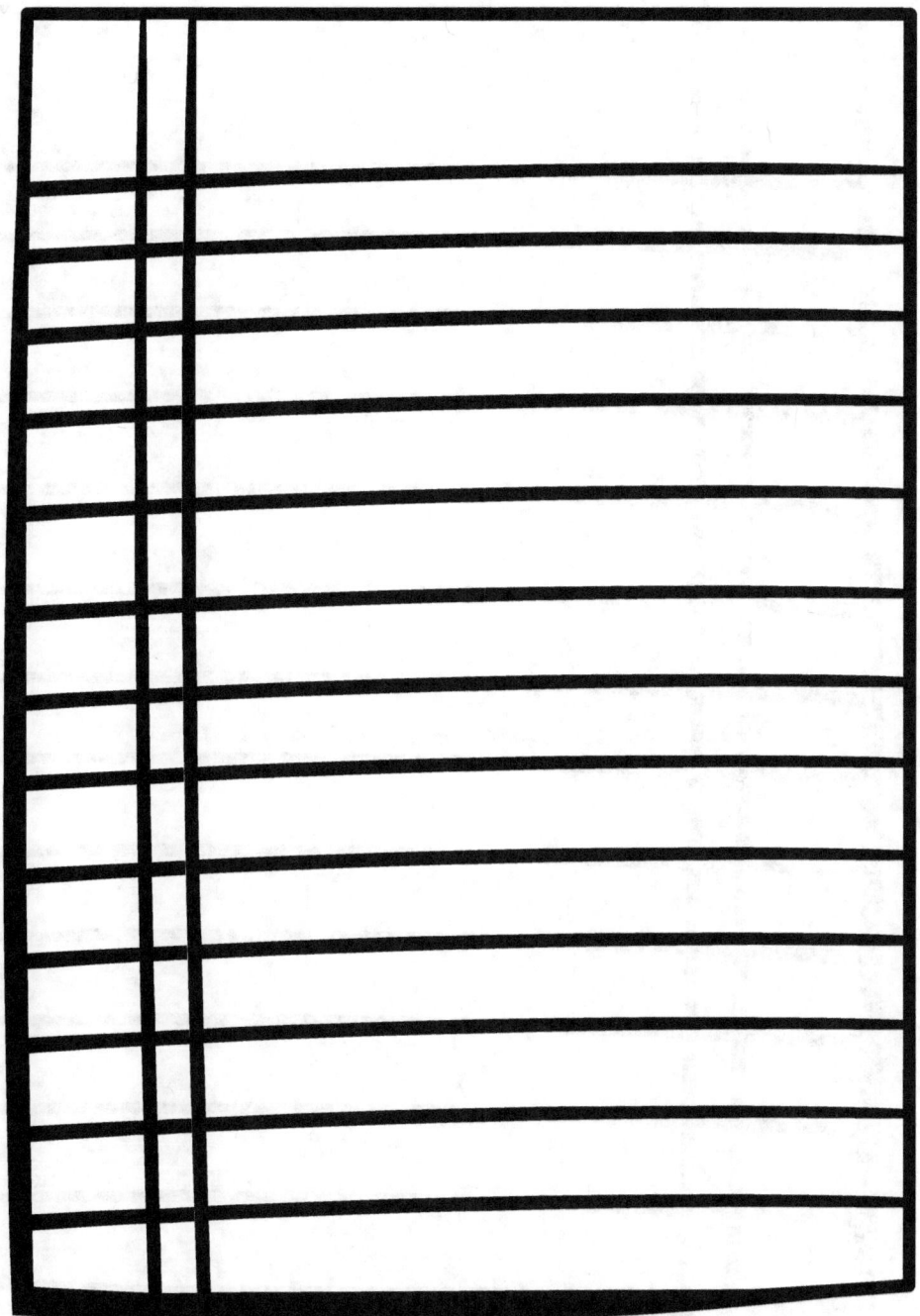

Notes:

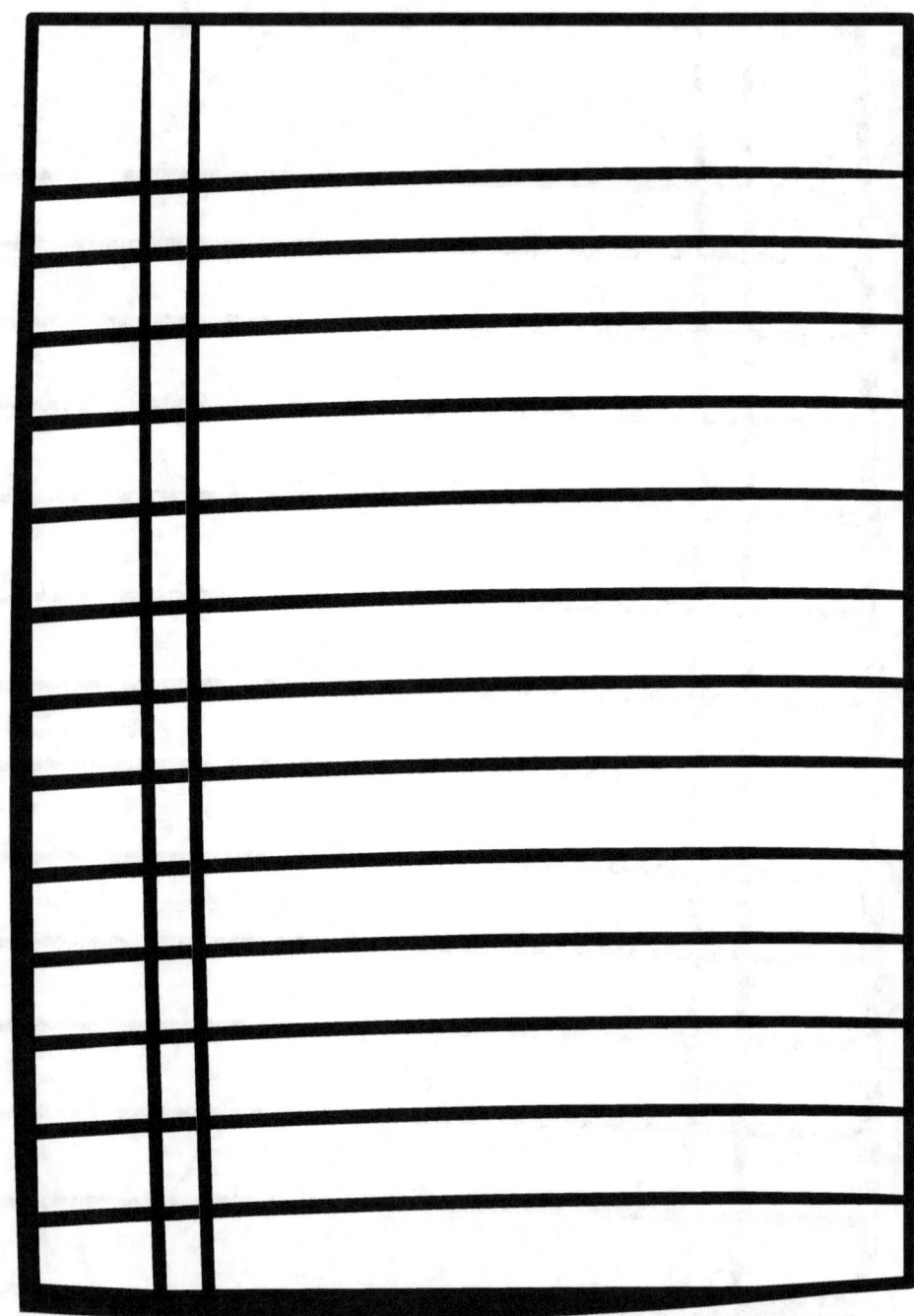

Did you know that your brain is like a muscle?
It changes and grows the more you use it. When you learn and practice, parts of your brain changes and gets stronger. You can train your brain through learning and practice!

I am good at...

I trained my brain to be good at it by...

I would like to become better at...

I can train my brain to be better by...

What challenge did you work out today?

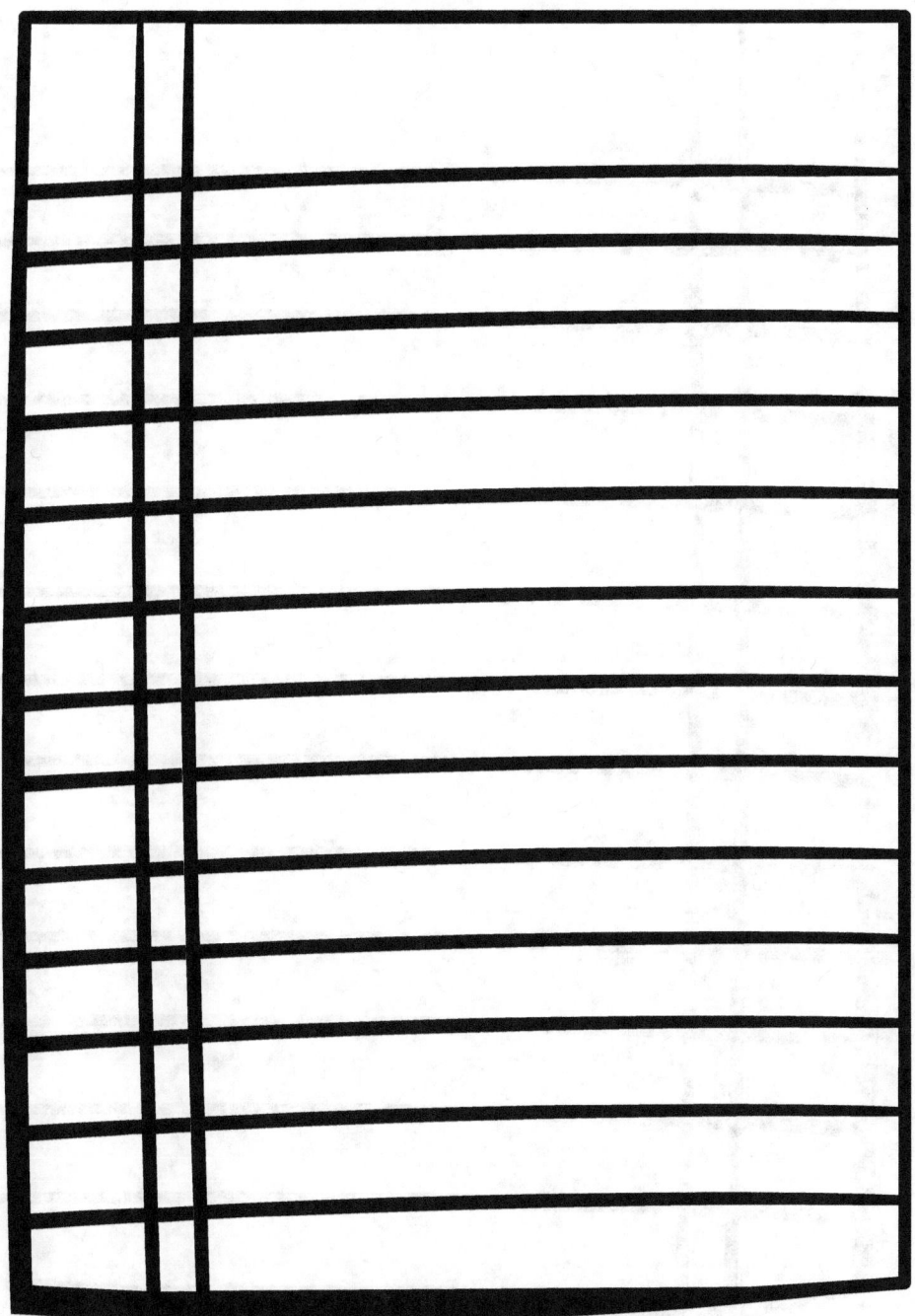

What did you learn today?

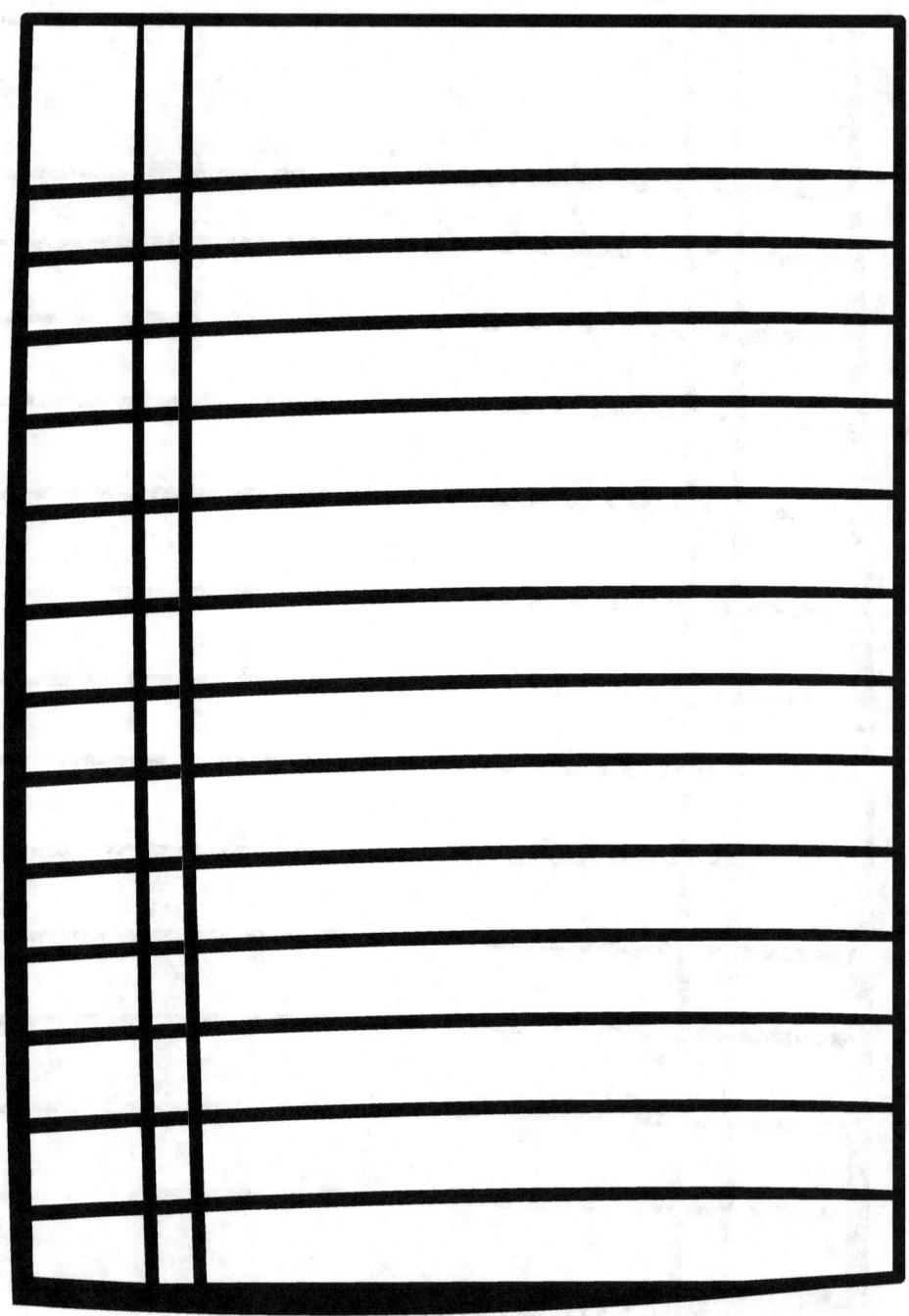

What did you learn today?

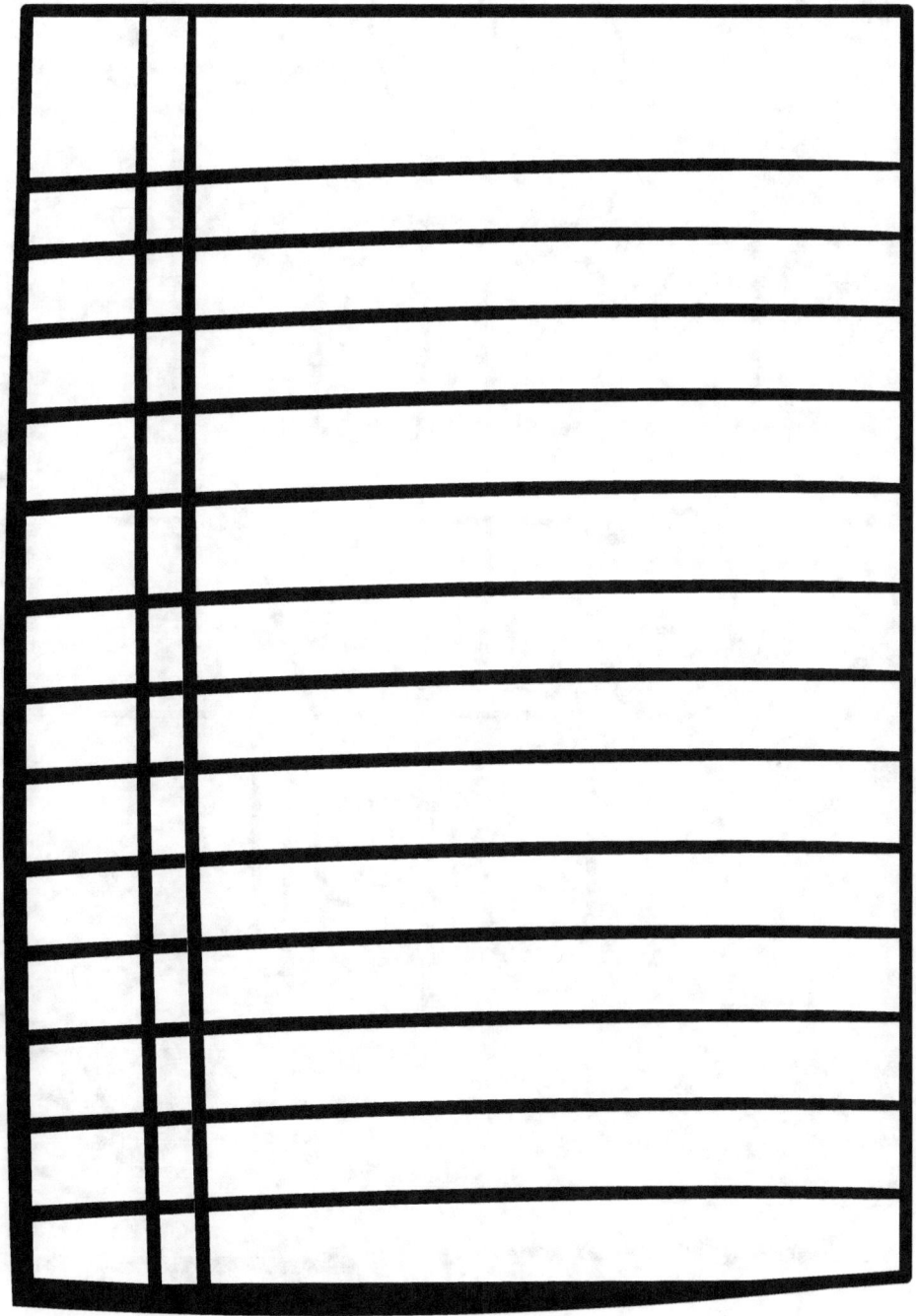

What did you learn today?

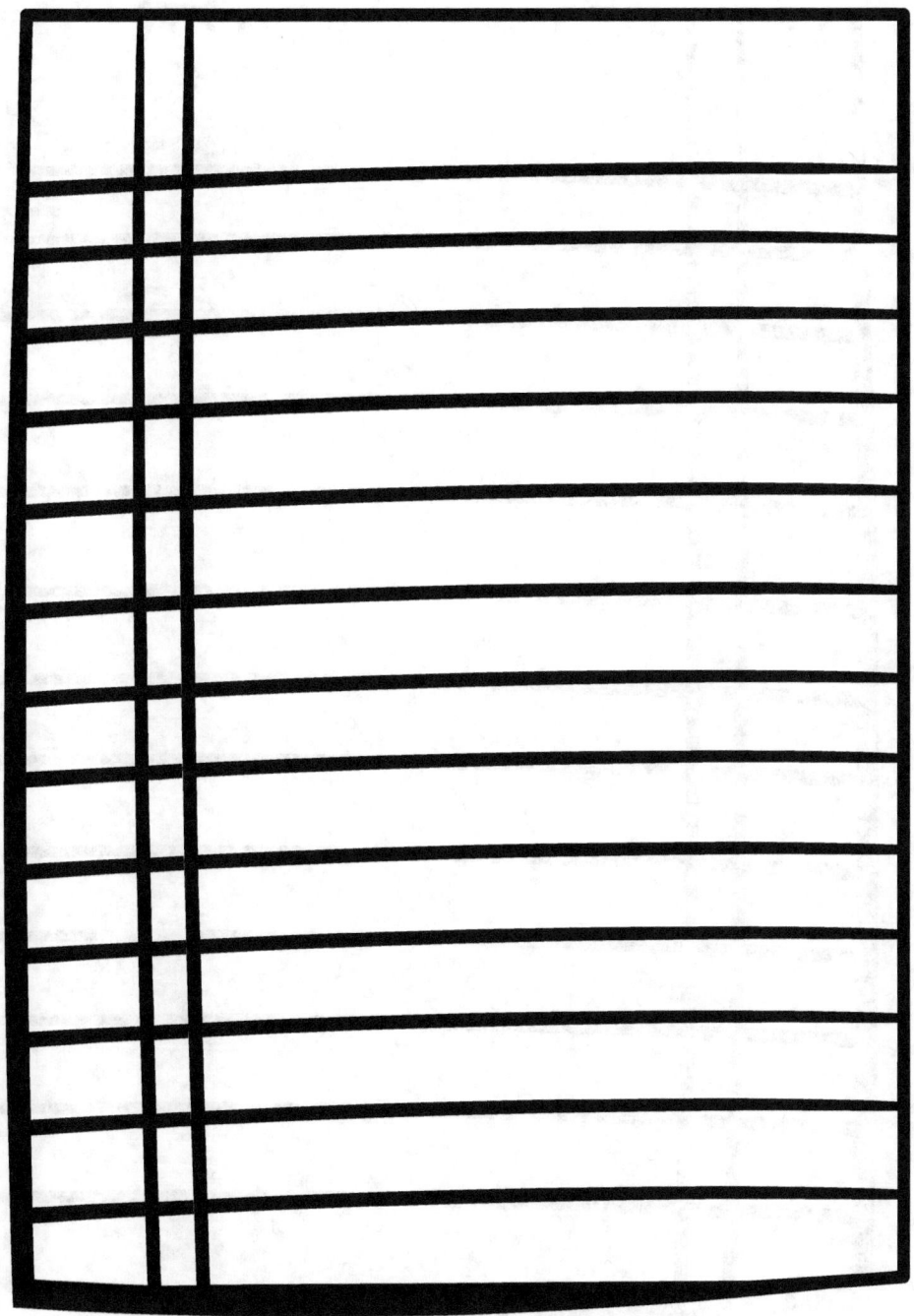

What did you learn today?

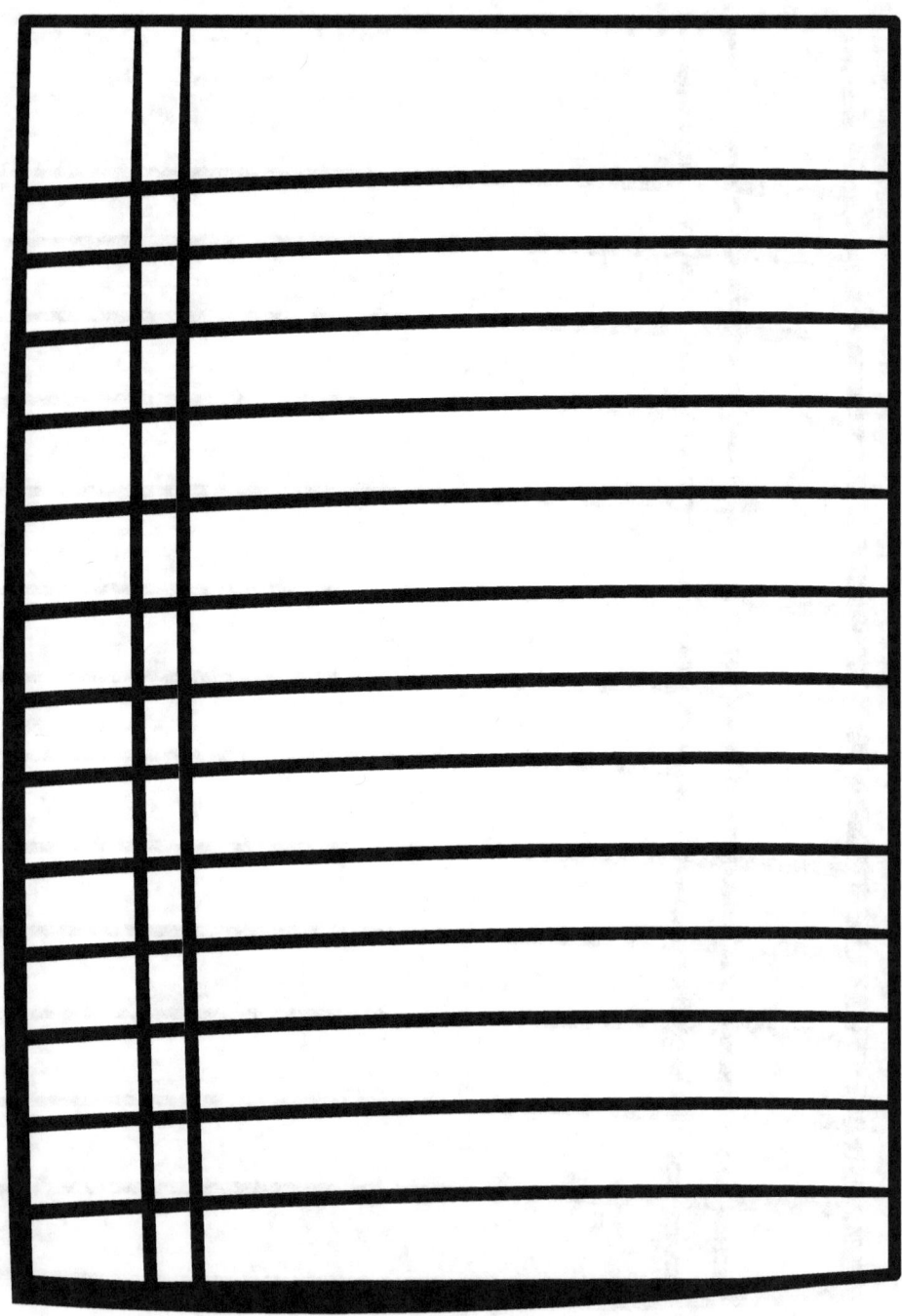

What did you learn today?

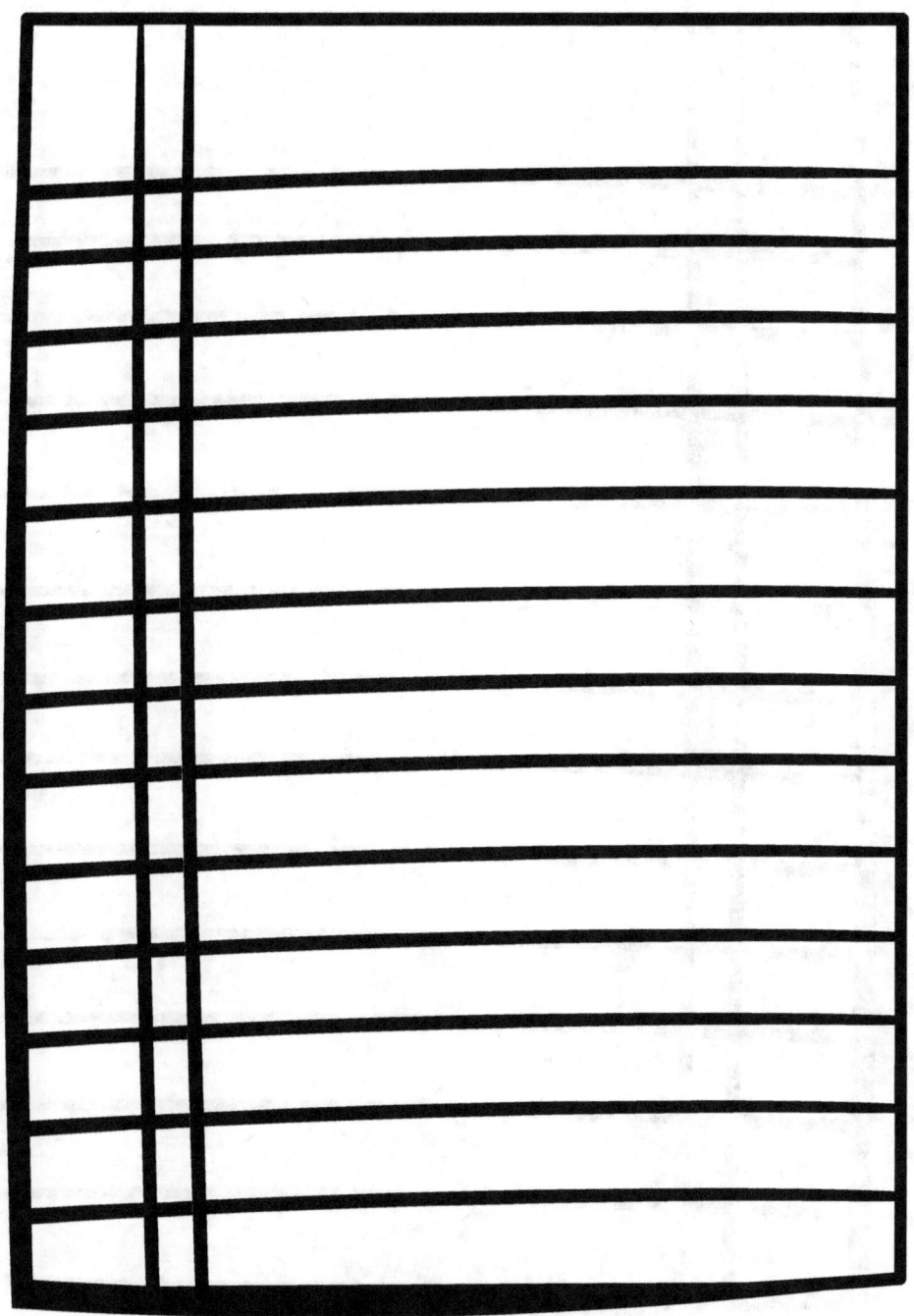

What did you learn today?

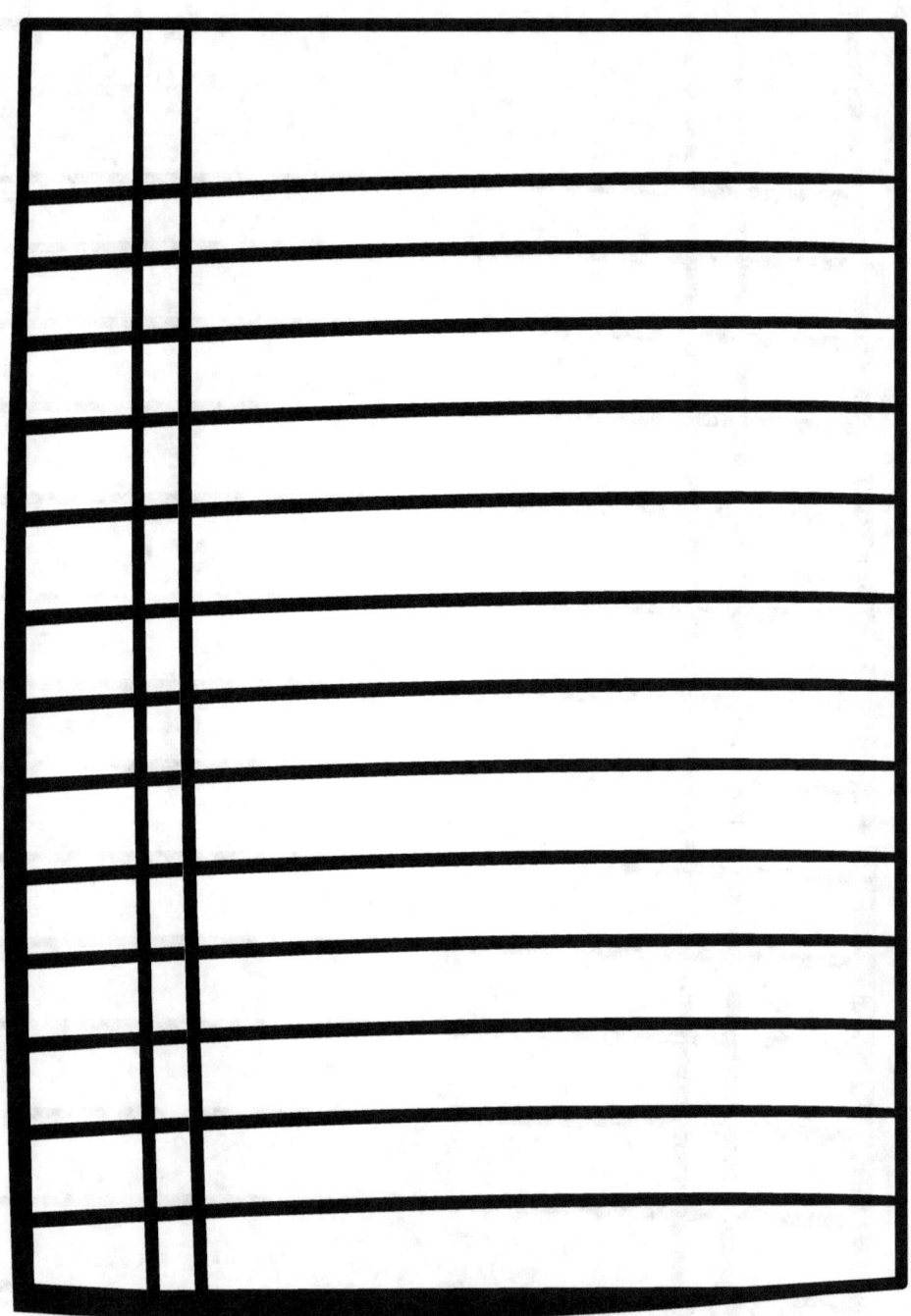

What did you learn today?

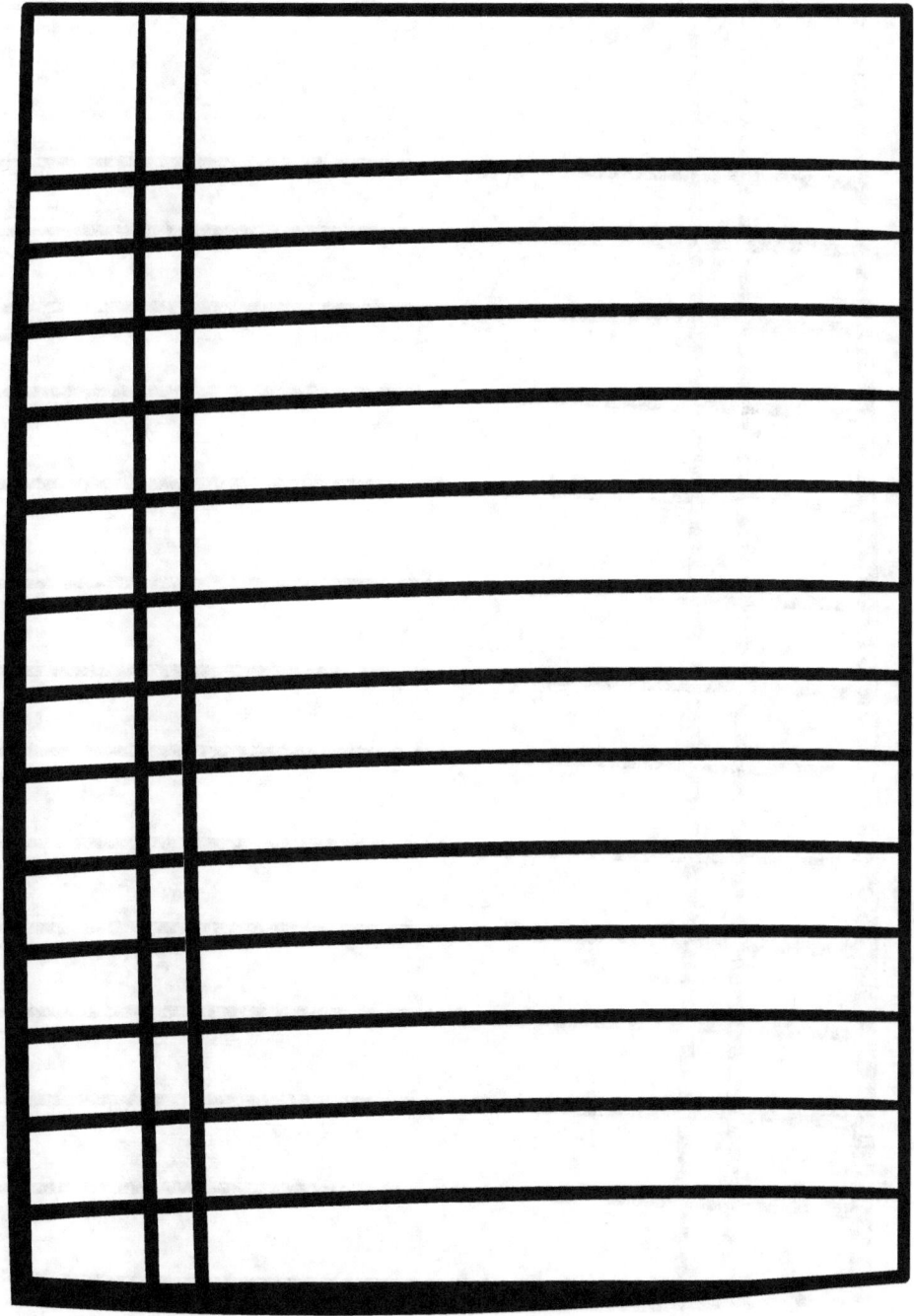

What did you learn today?

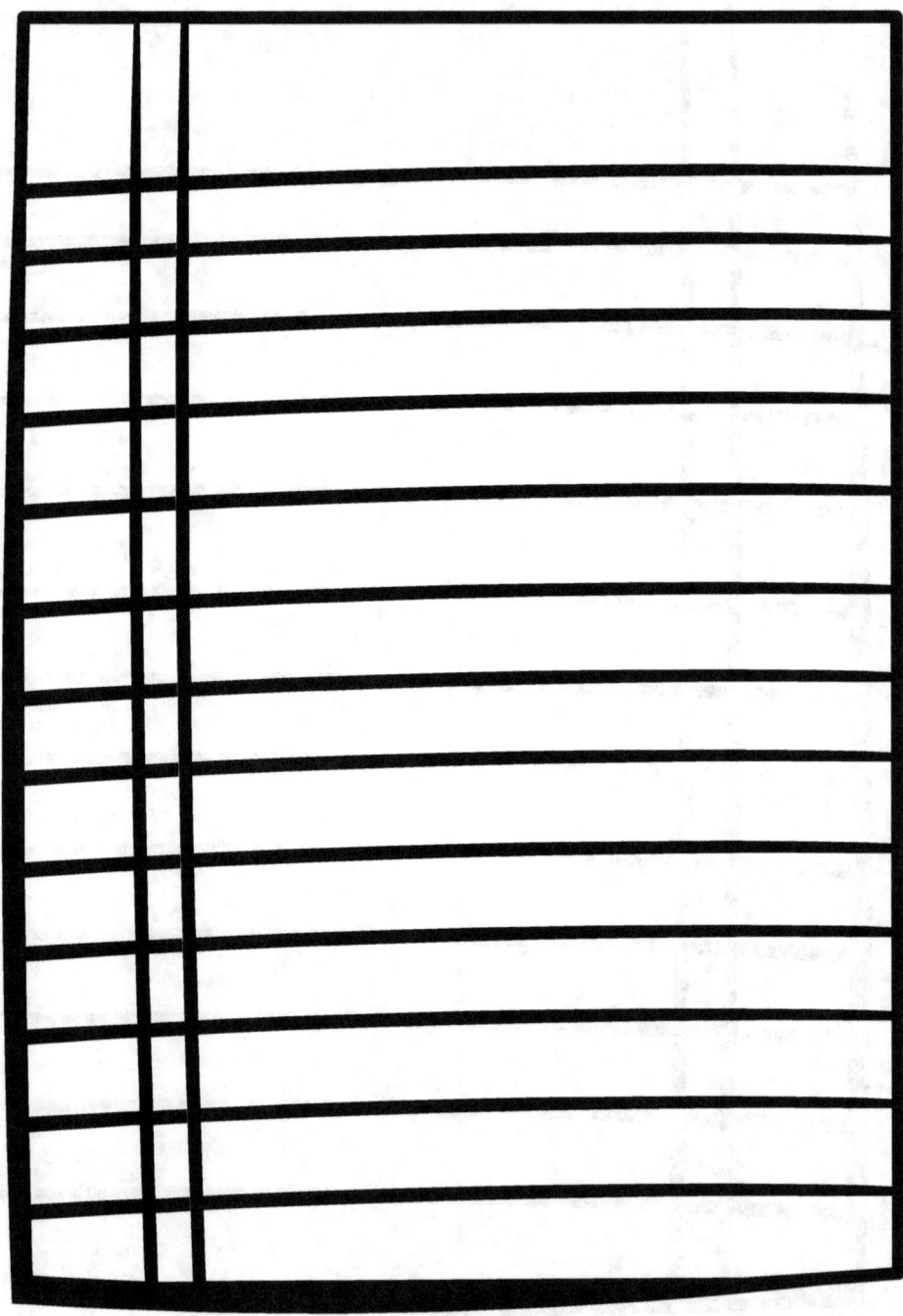

What did you learn today?

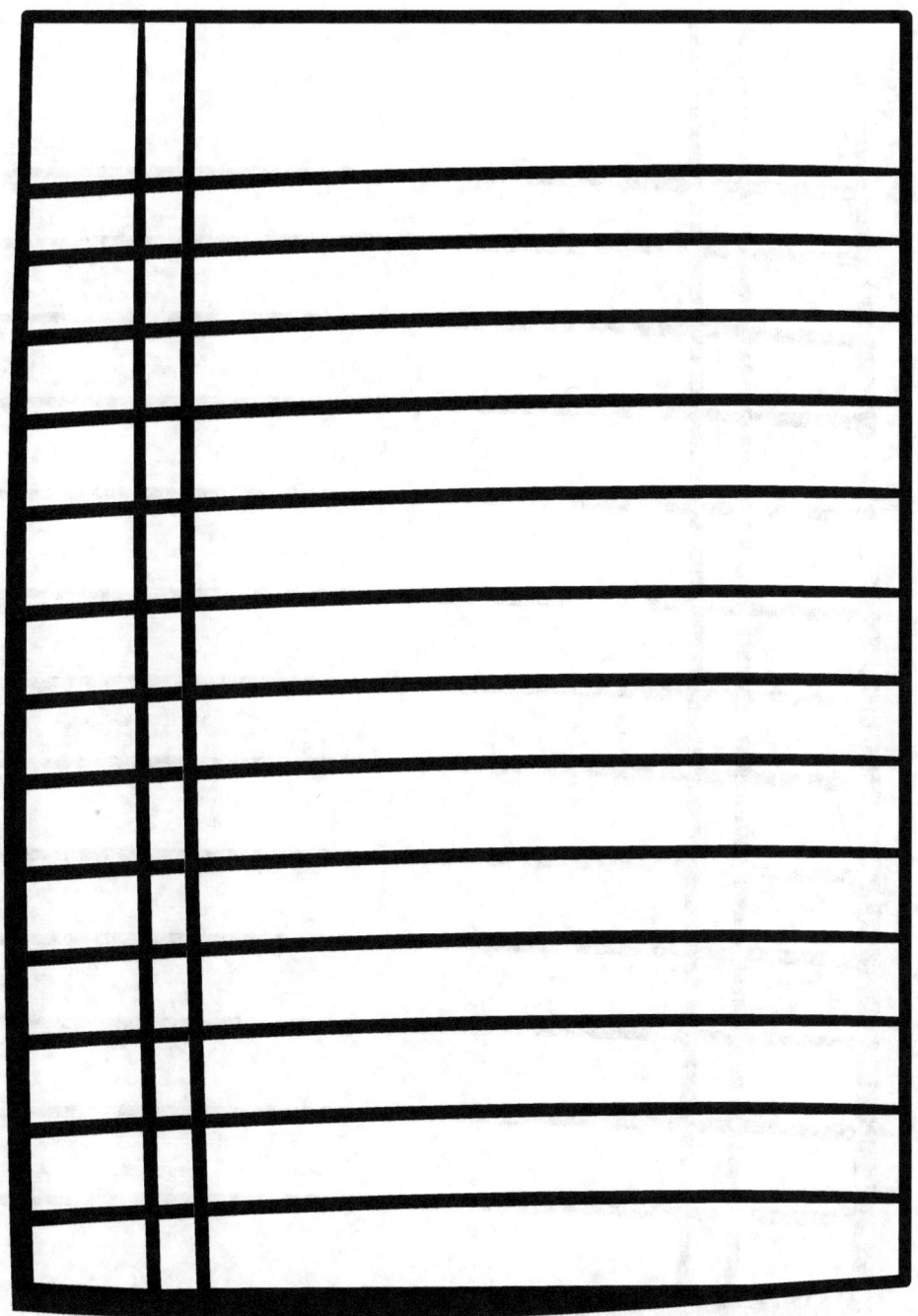

What did you learn today?

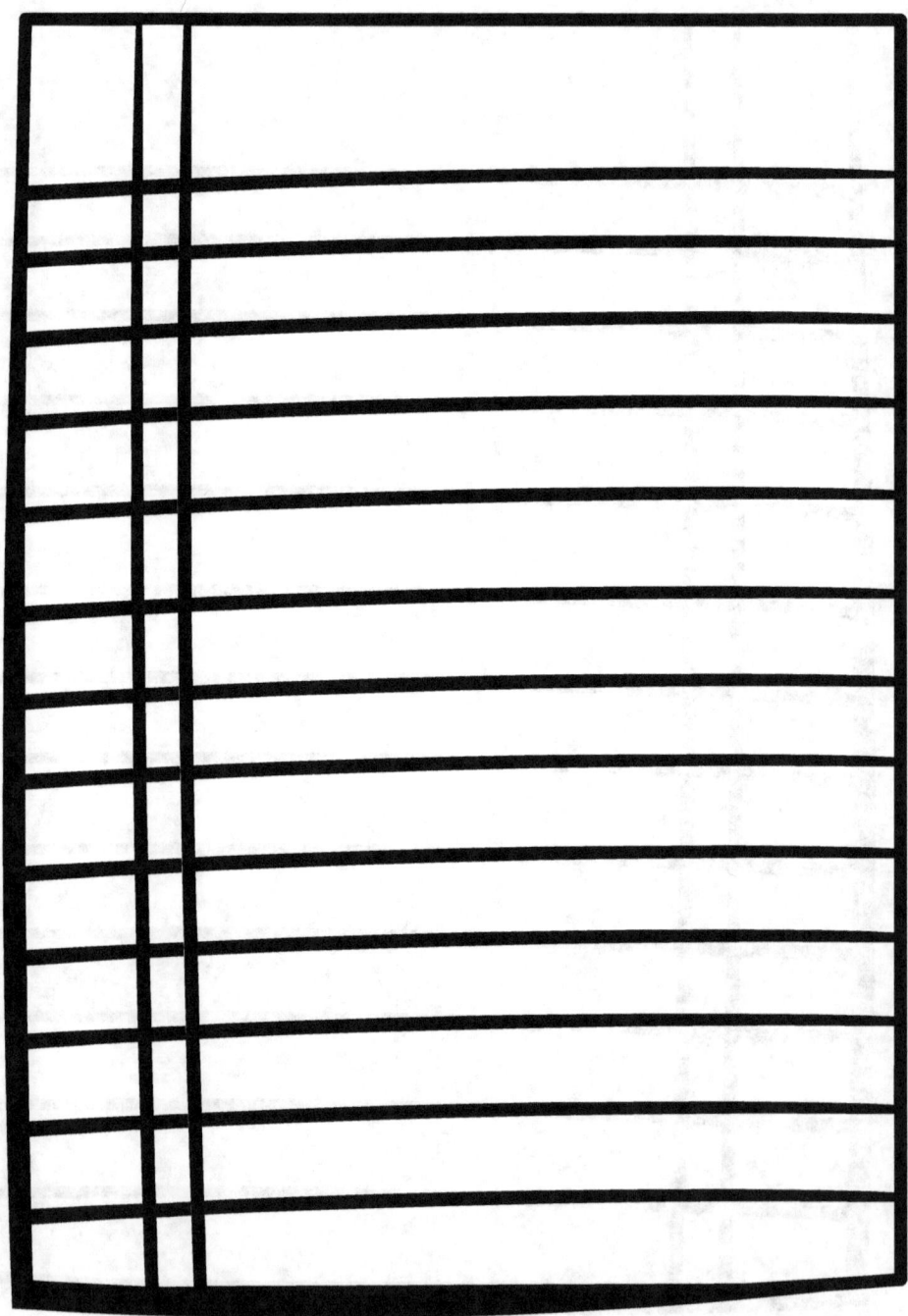

What did you learn today?

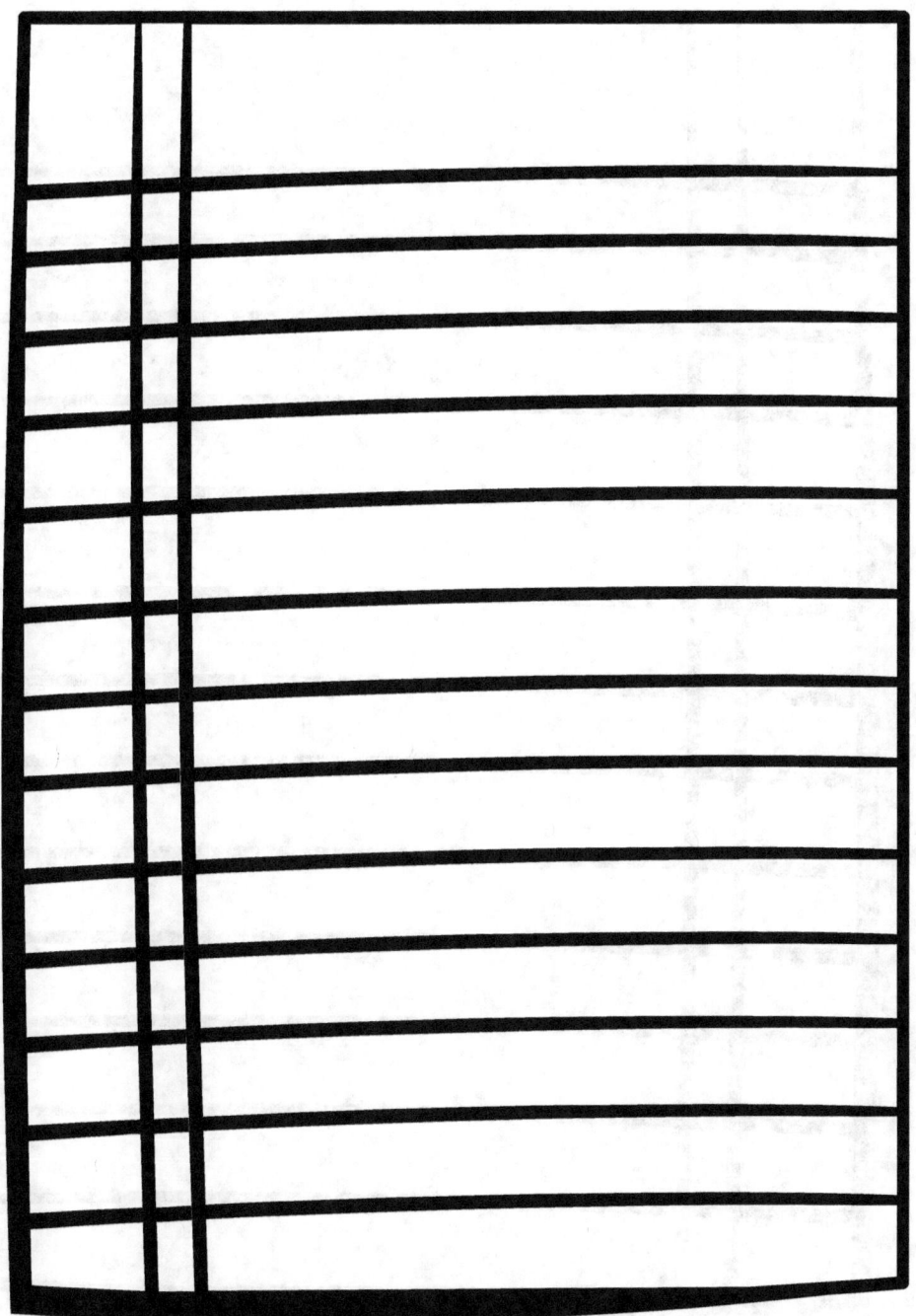

Notes:

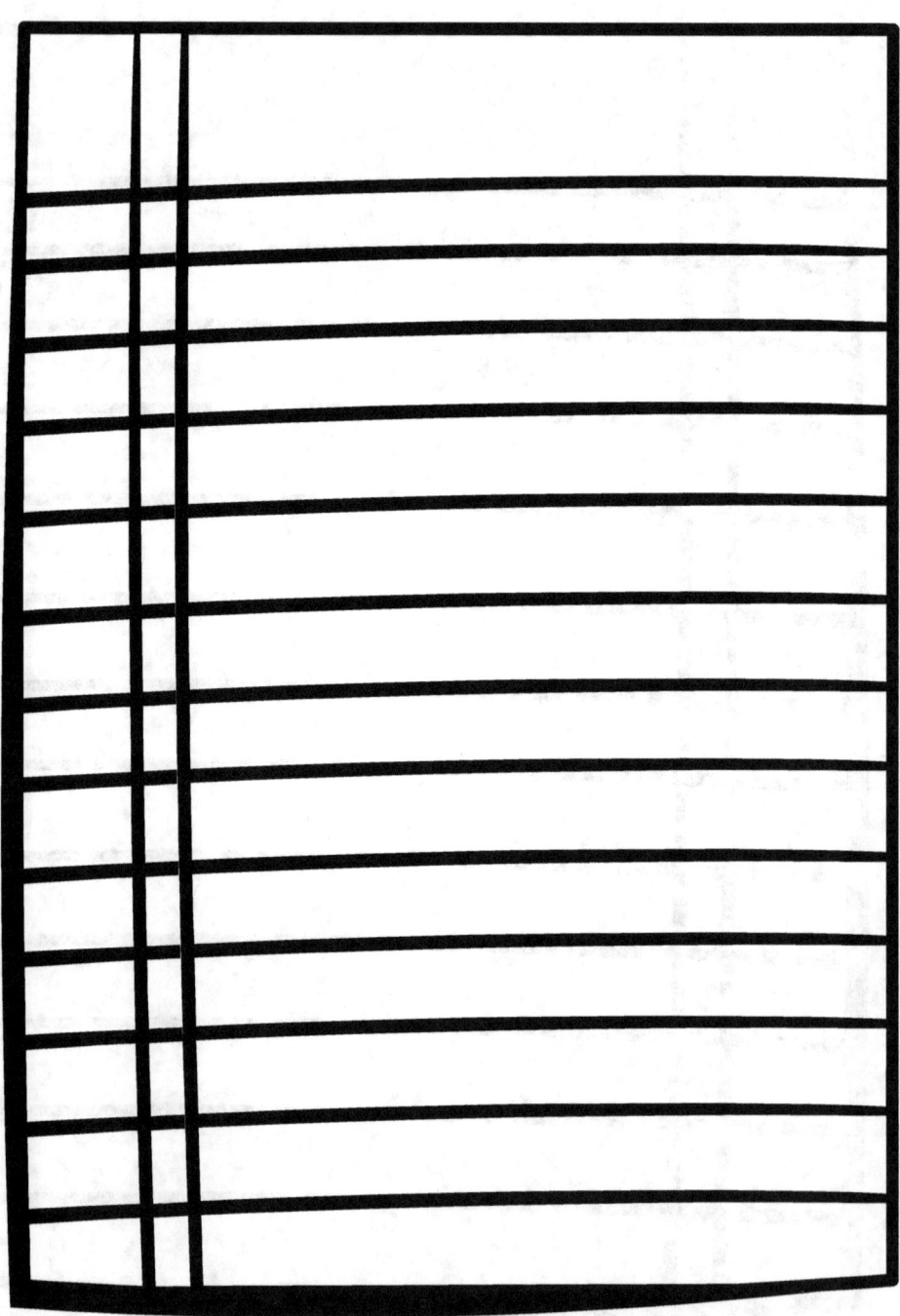

What makes you happy?

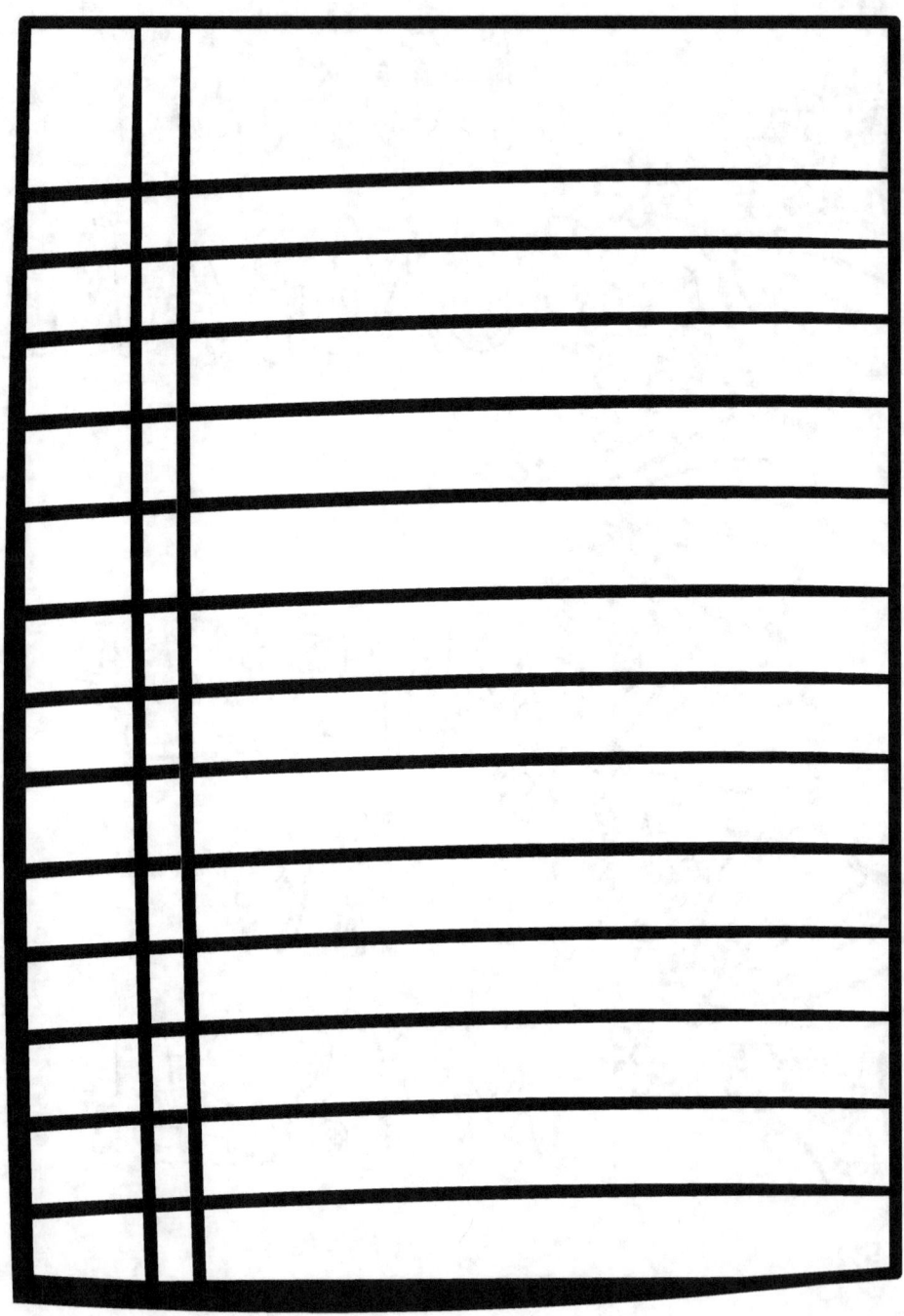

Notes:

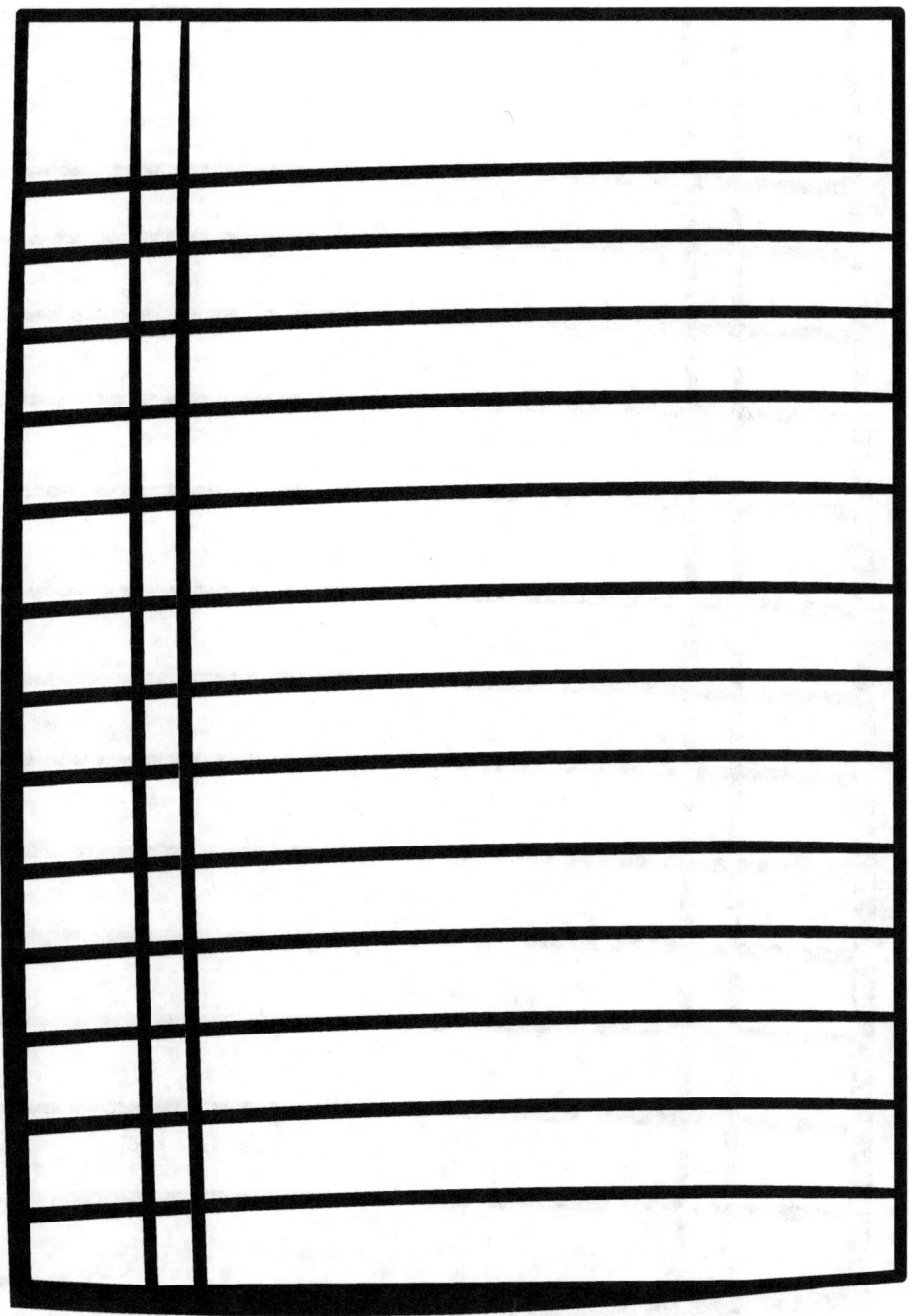

What makes you sad?

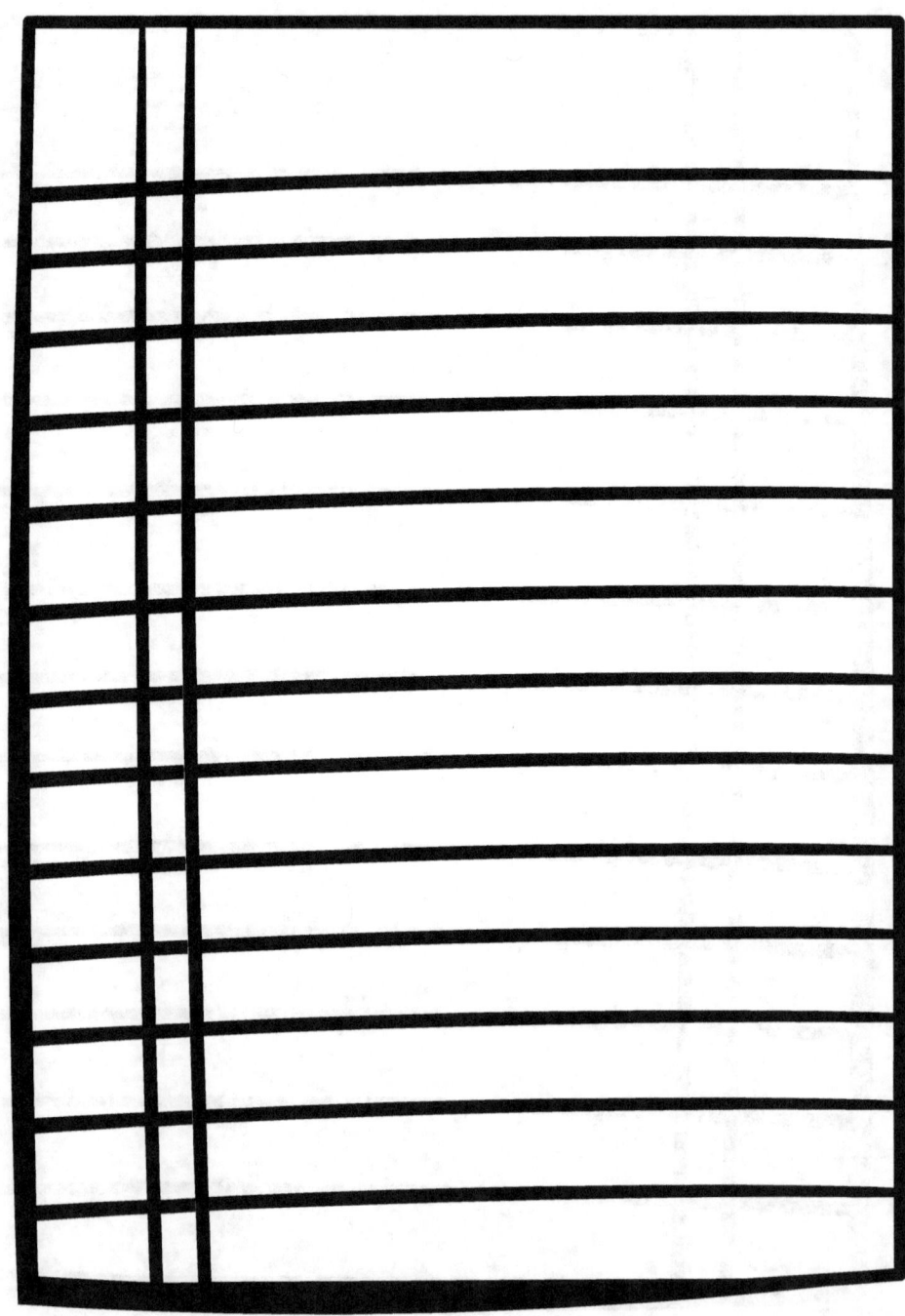

Notes:

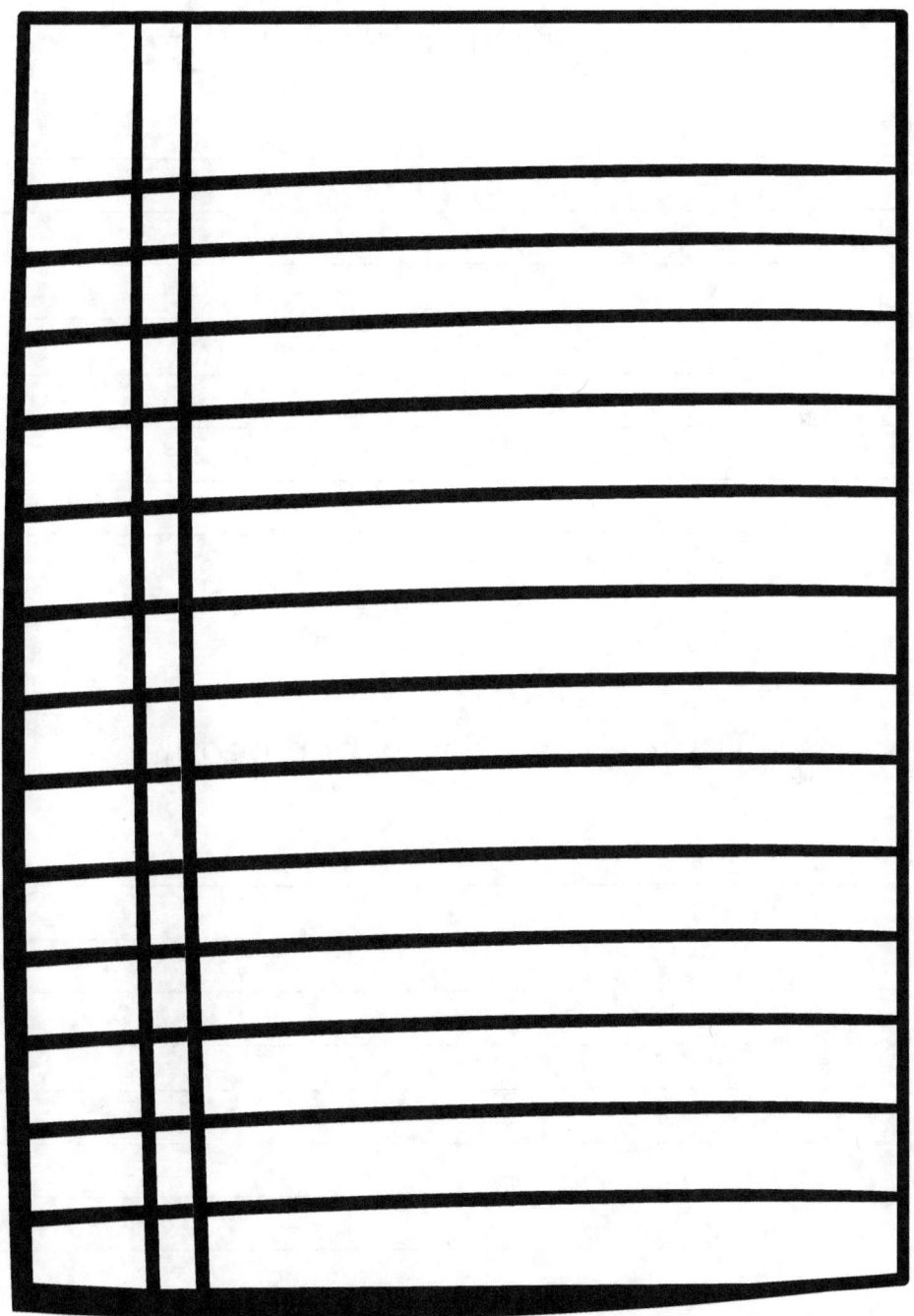

Acts of Kindess

Things people did for me:

_____
_____
_____
_____
_____
_____
_____

Things I did for other people:

_____
_____
_____
_____
_____
_____
_____

Who is one person that you look up to and why?

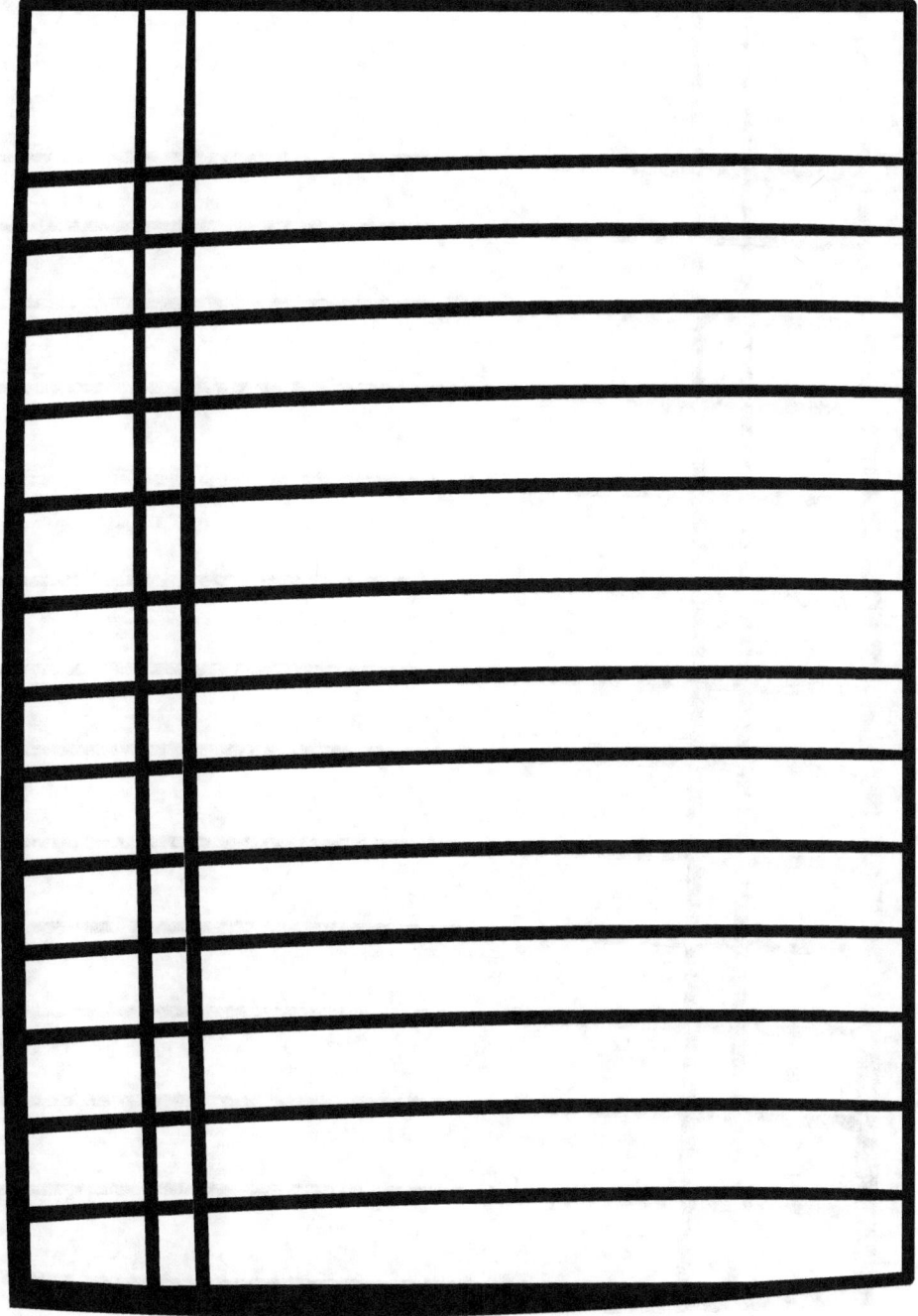

Notes:

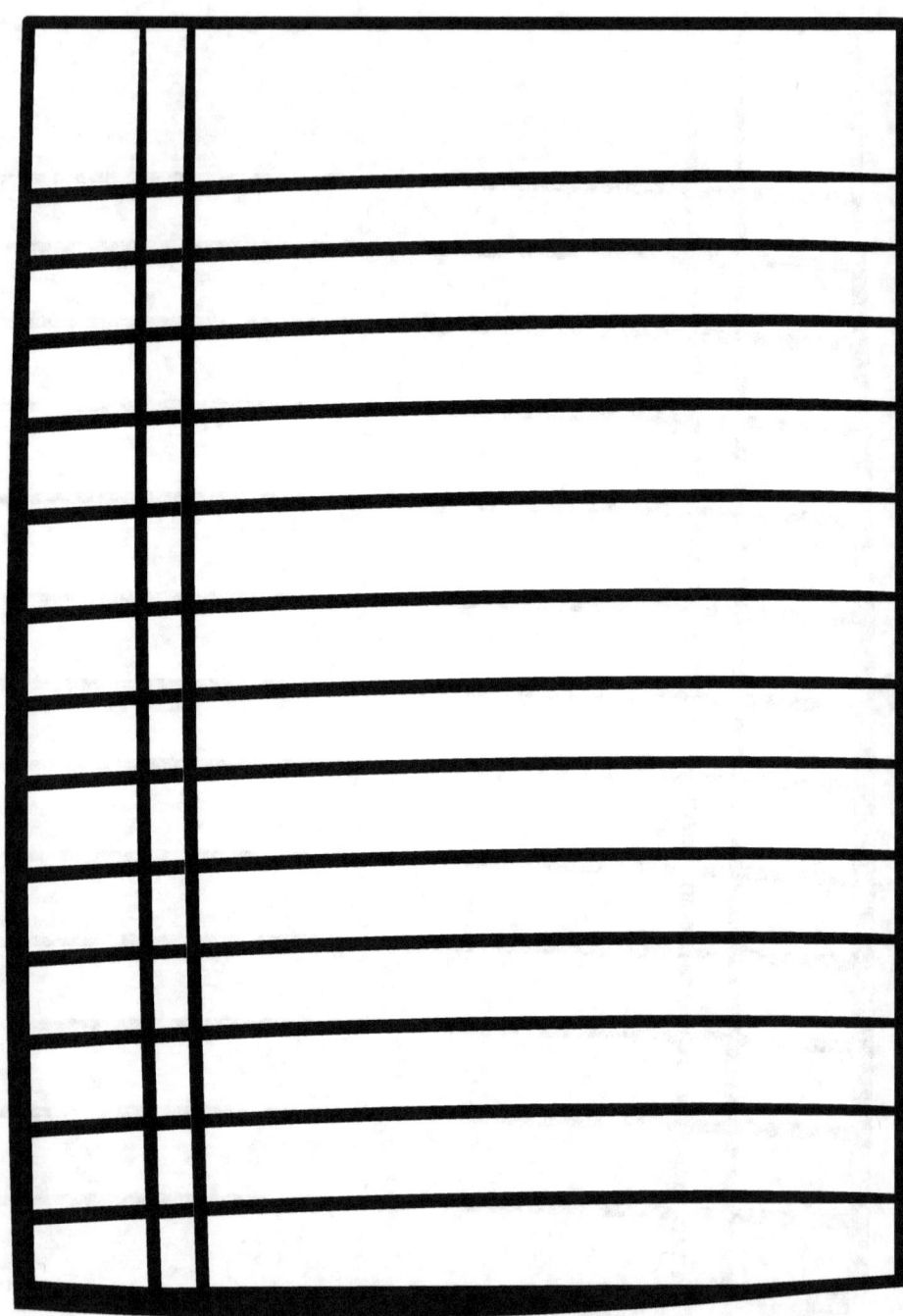

I TURN MY CAN'TS INTO CANS

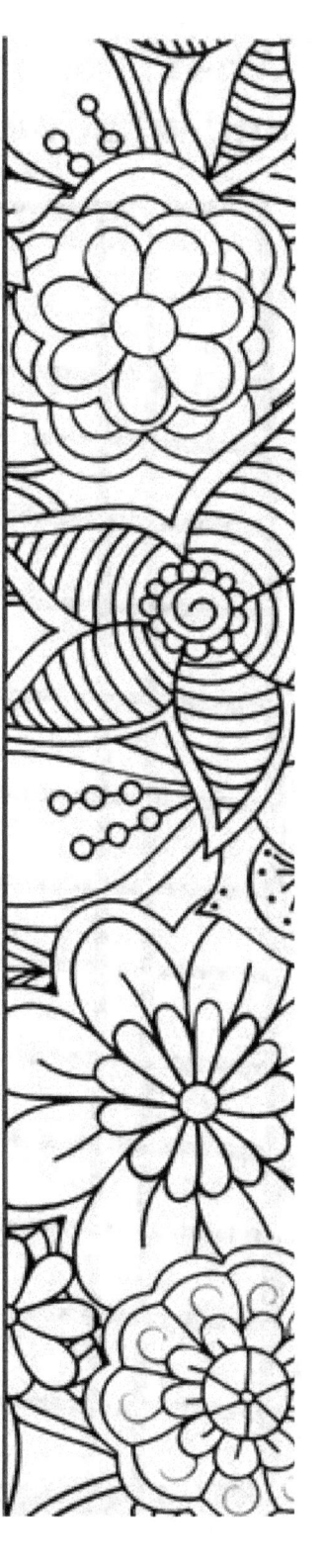

What is one mistake you made today and what did you learn from it?

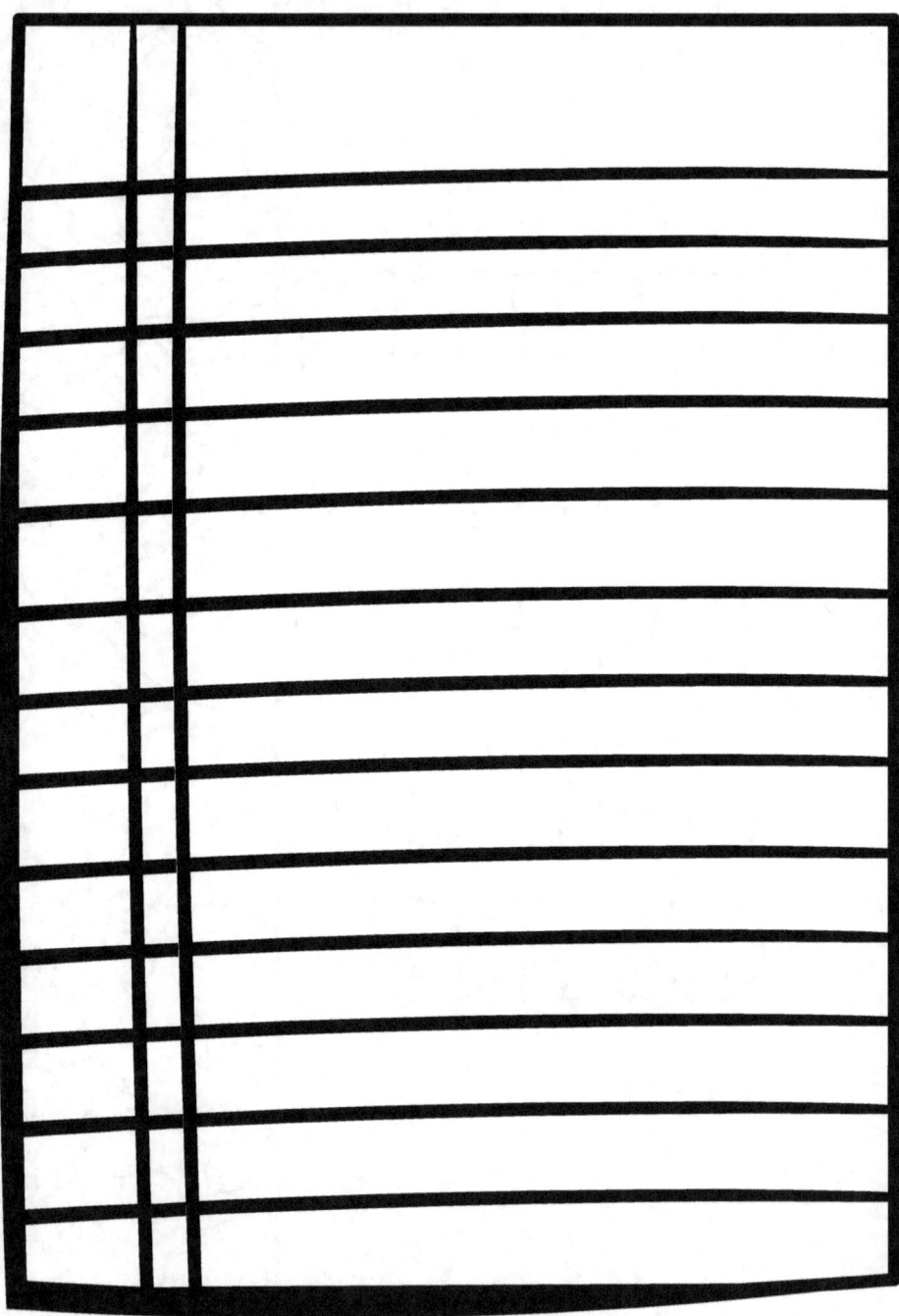

What is one mistake you made today and what did you learn from it?

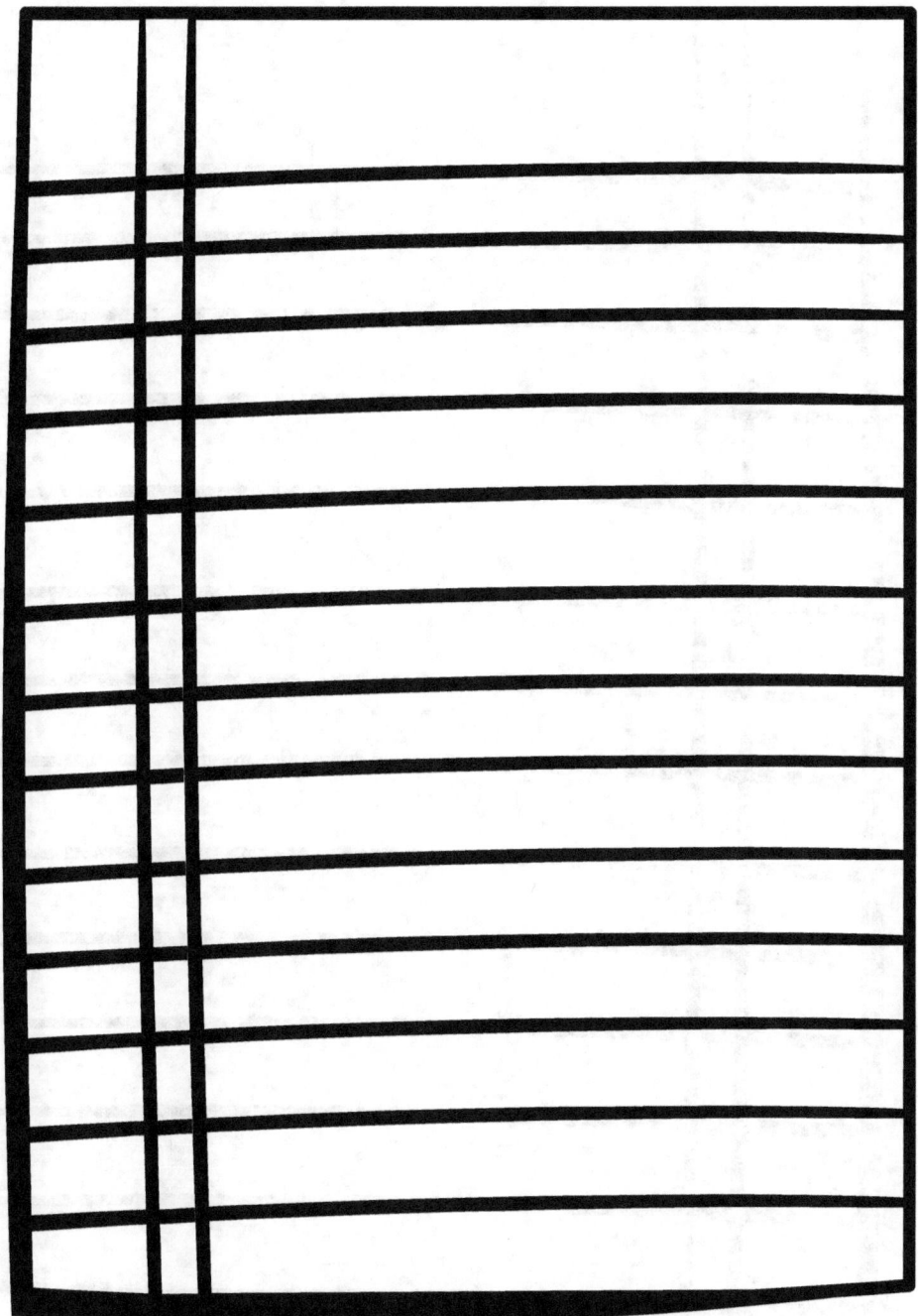

What is one mistake you made today and what did you learn from it?

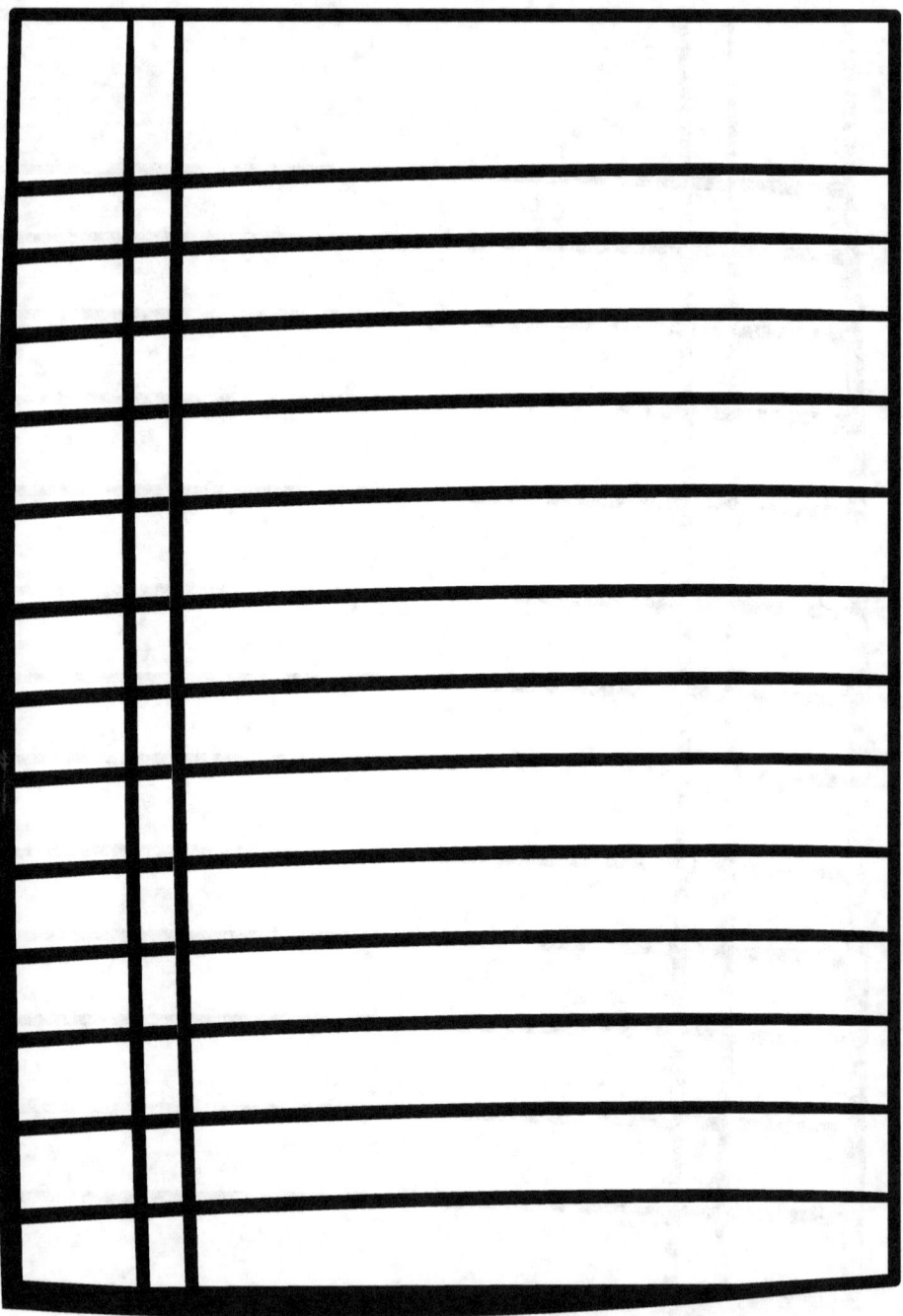

What is one mistake you made today and what did you learn from it?

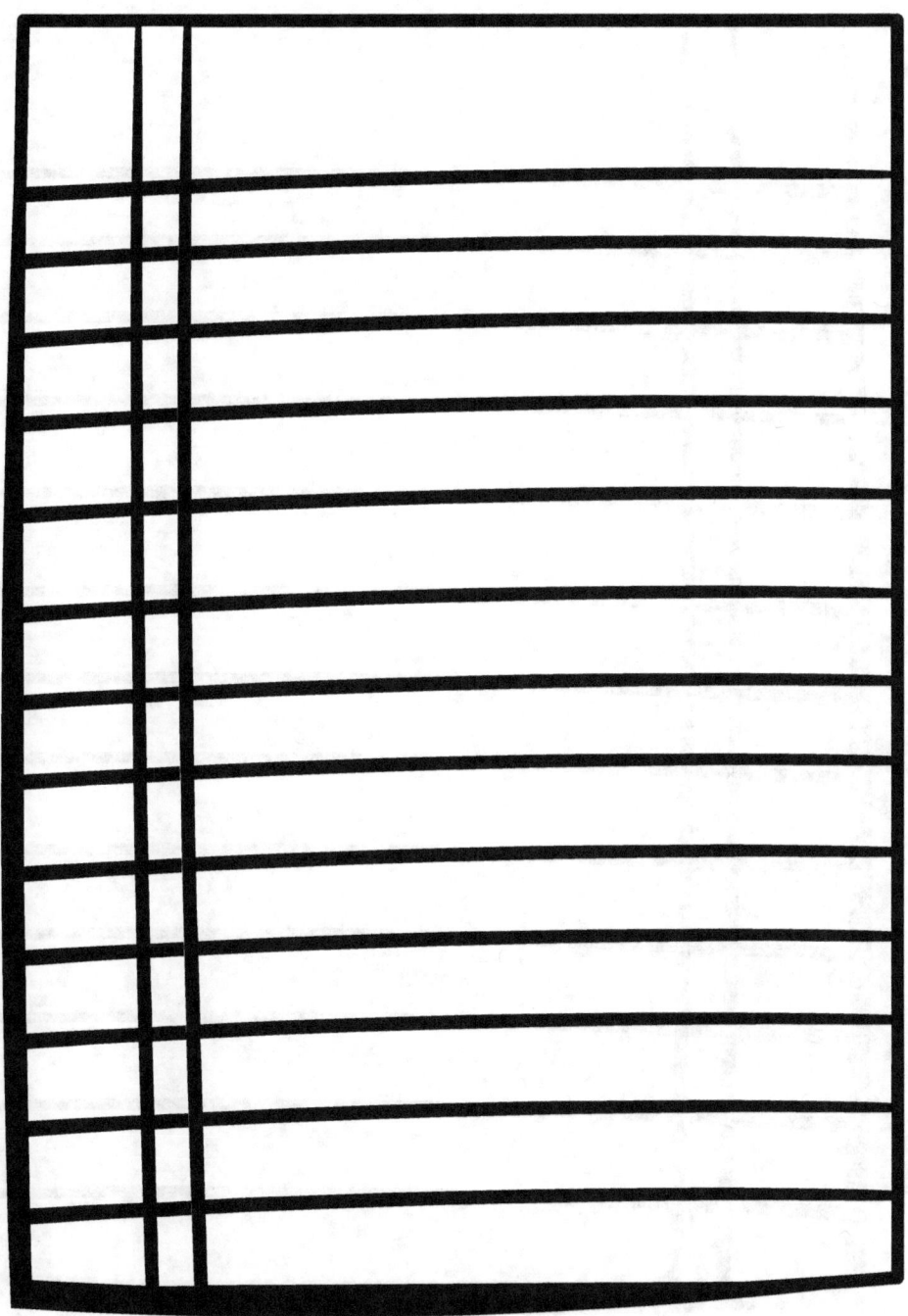

What is one mistake you made today and what did you learn from it?

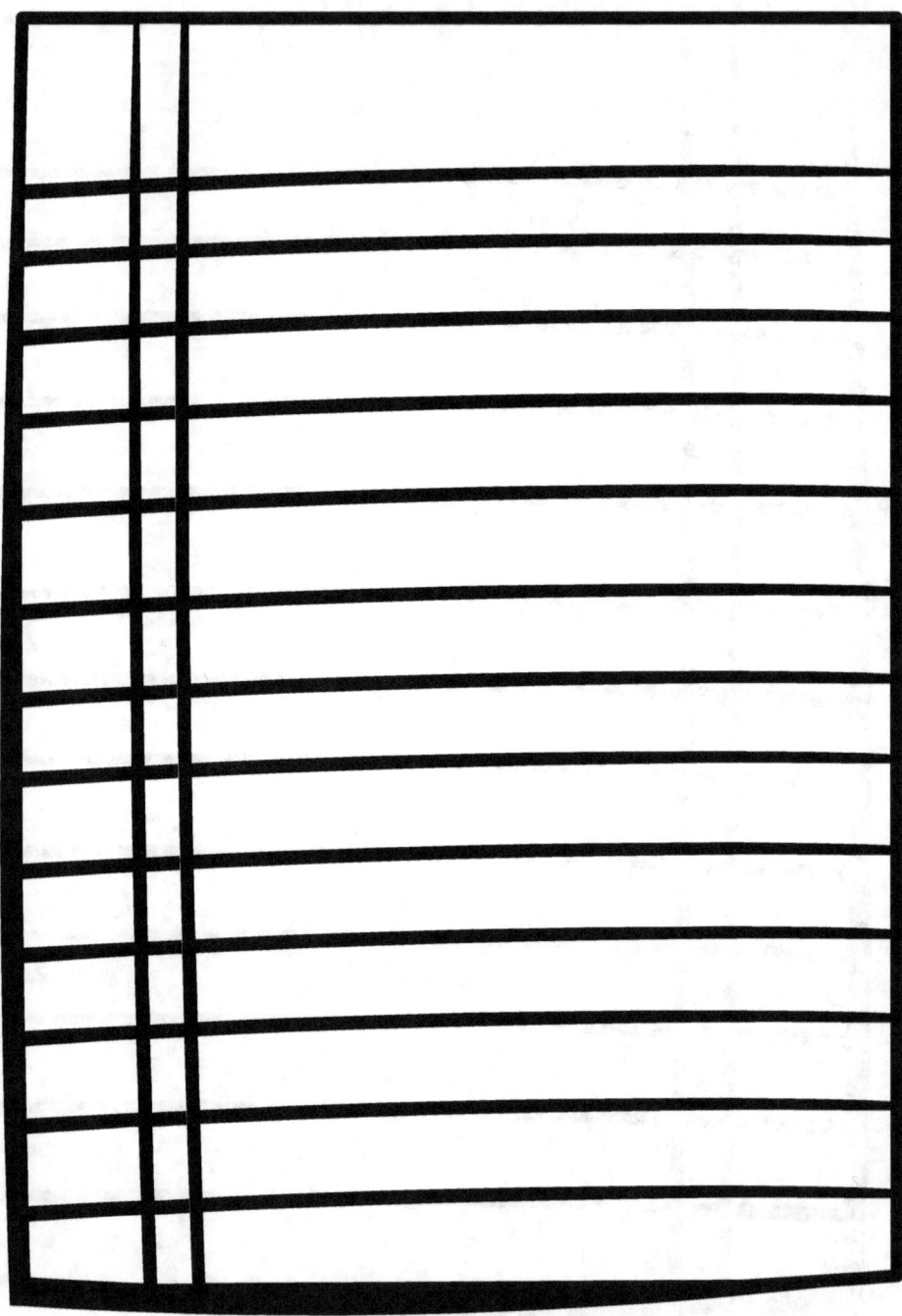

What is one mistake you made today and what did you learn from it?

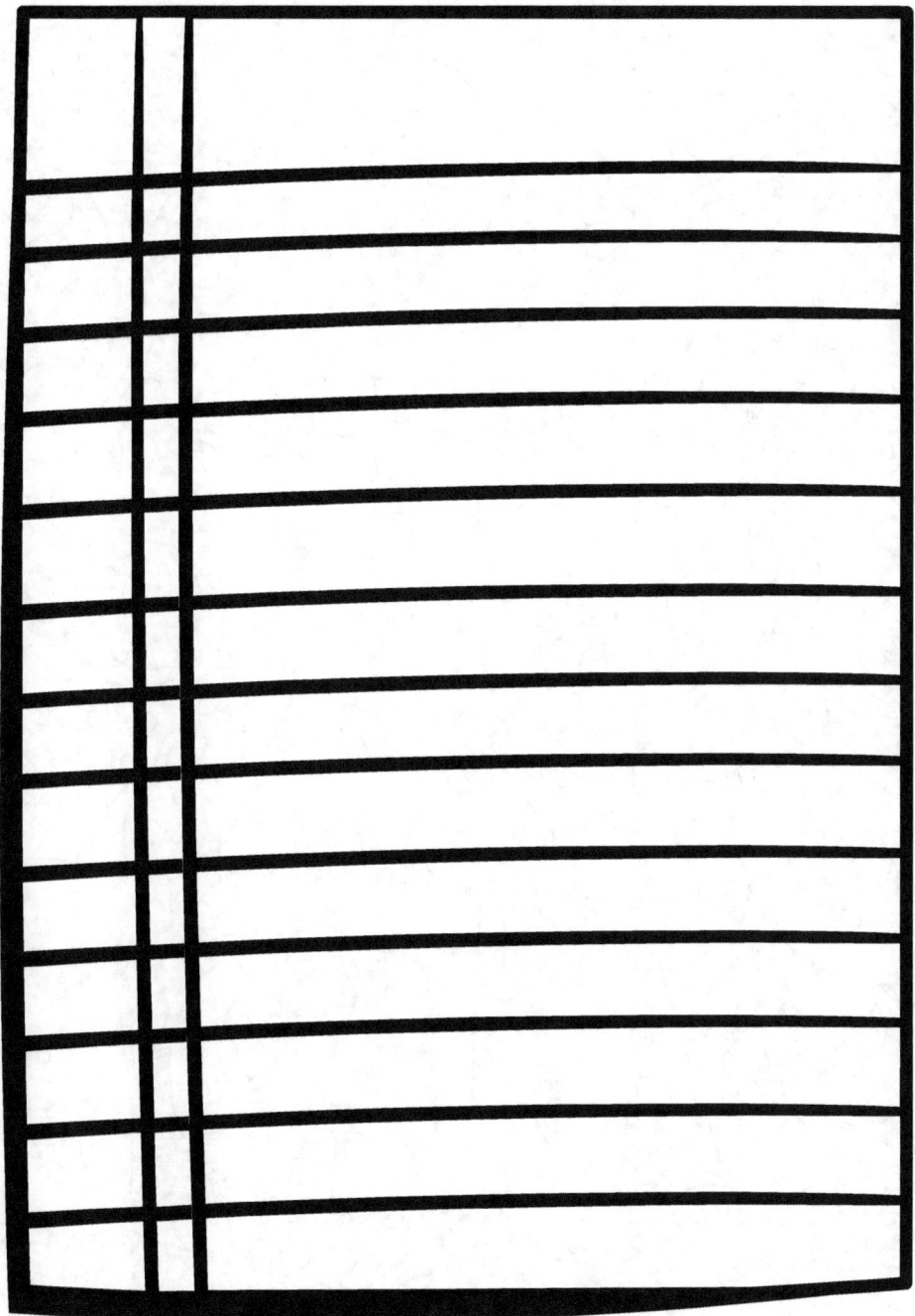

What are three things you're grateful for?

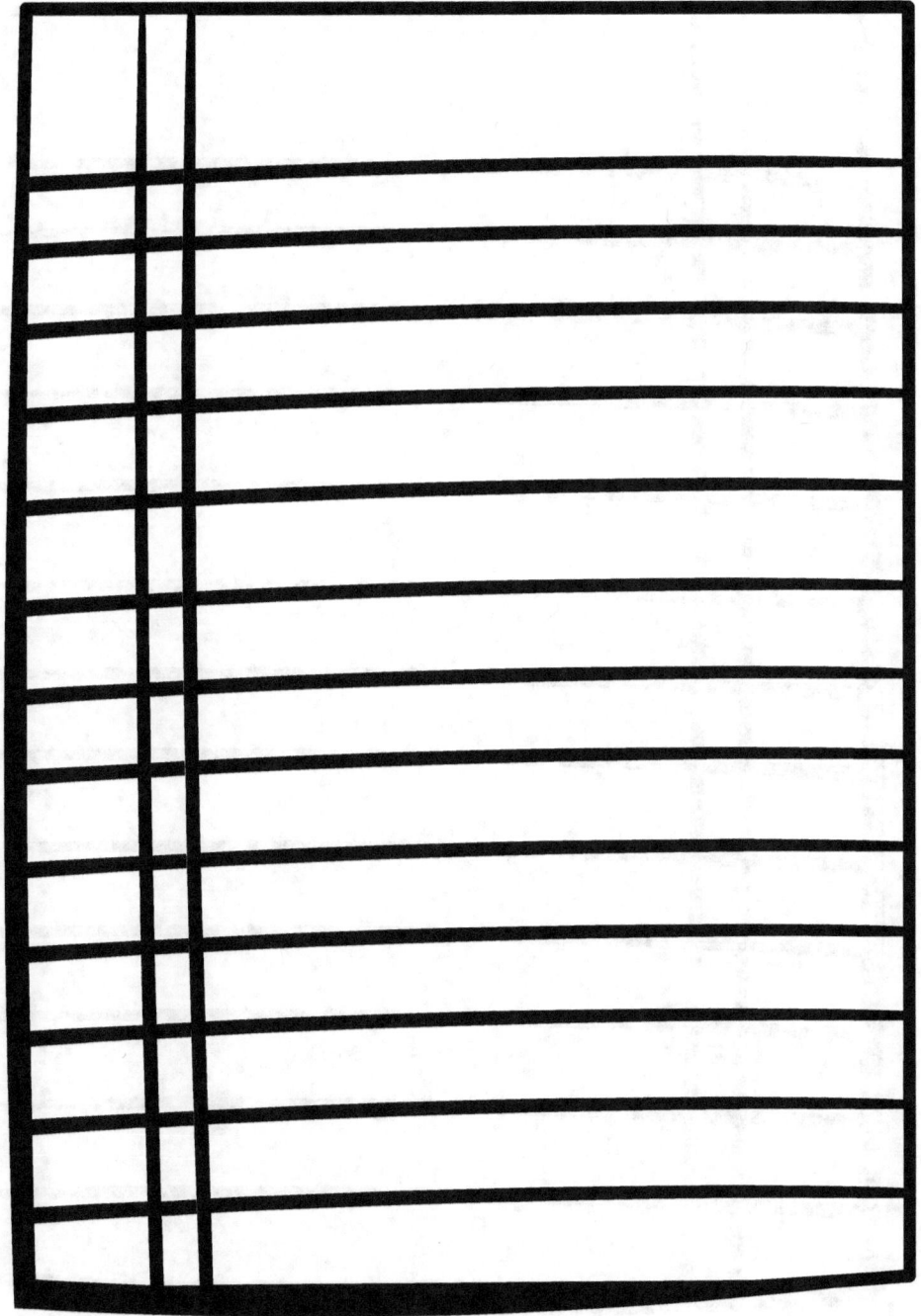

Notes:

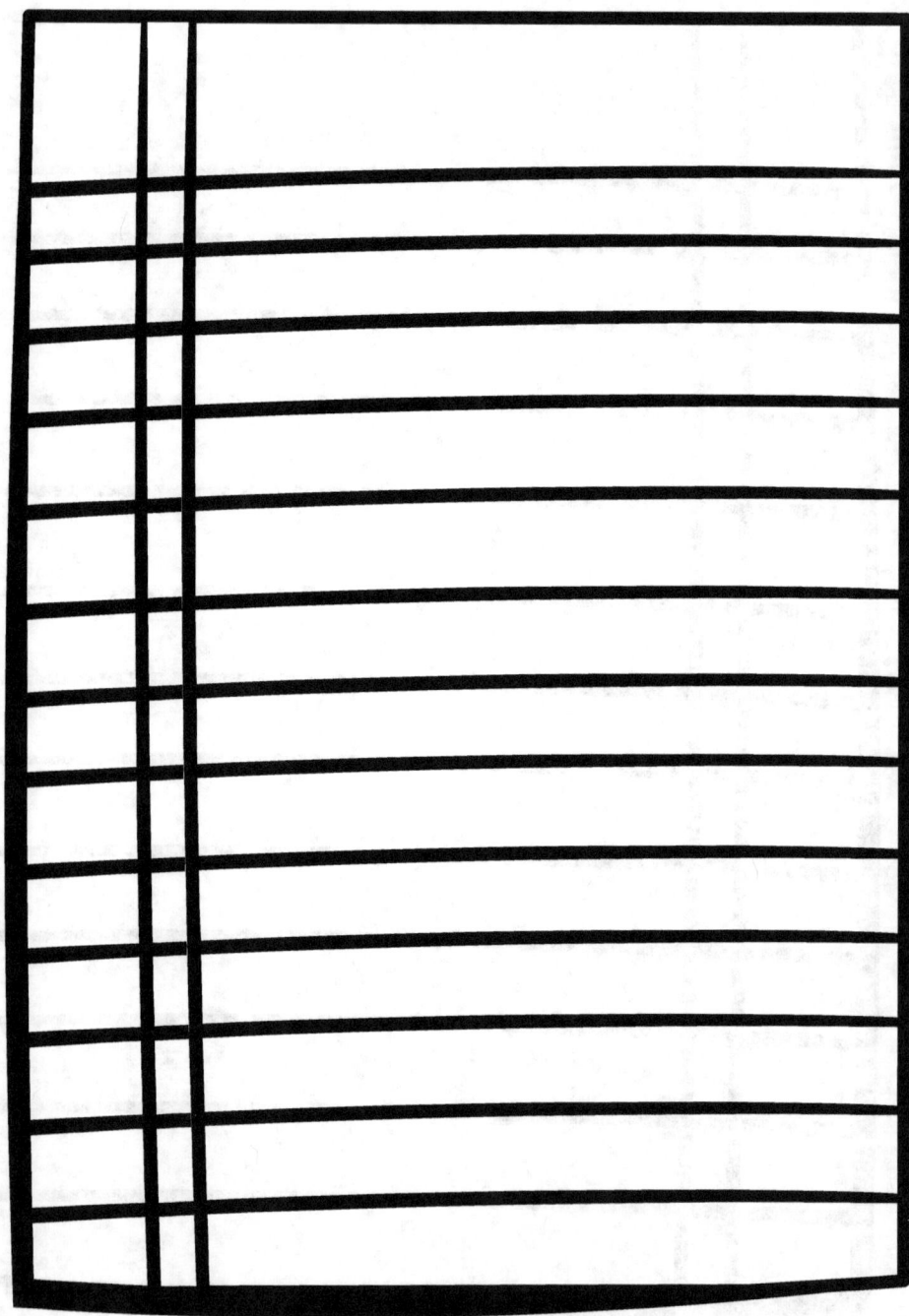

If you could spend one day doing anything you want, what would you do?

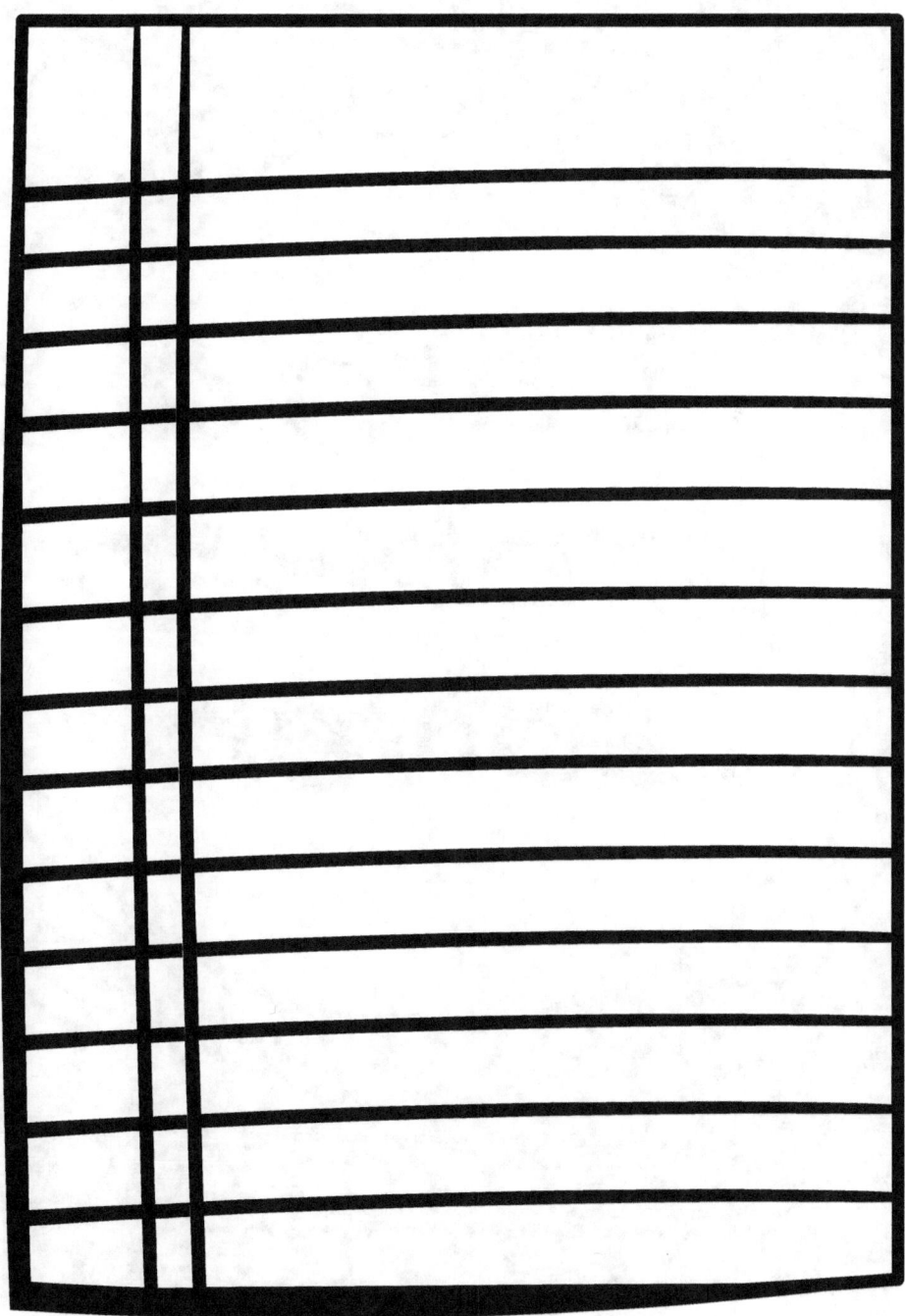

Name three things that you want to be good at.

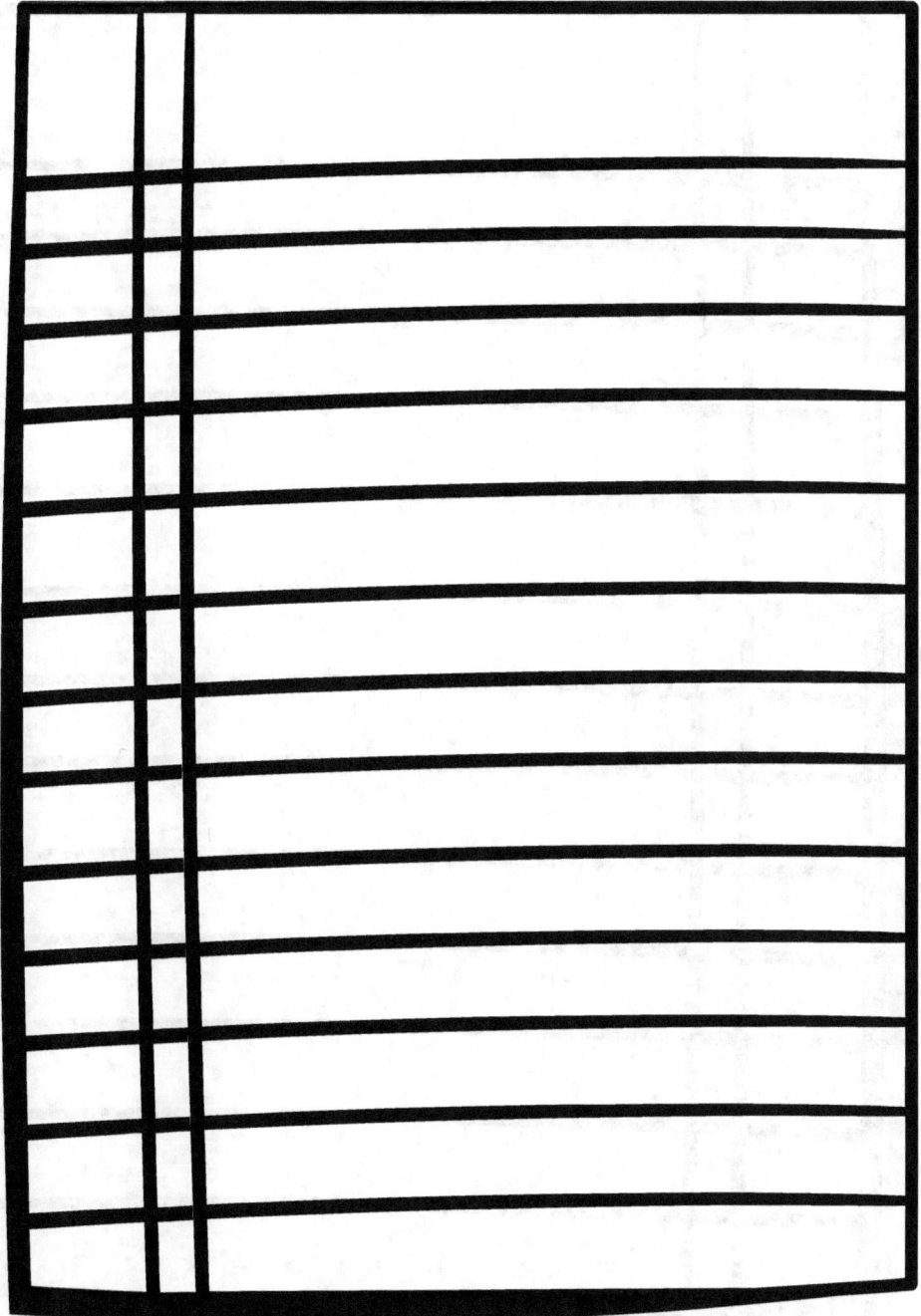

What will you do to be good at them?

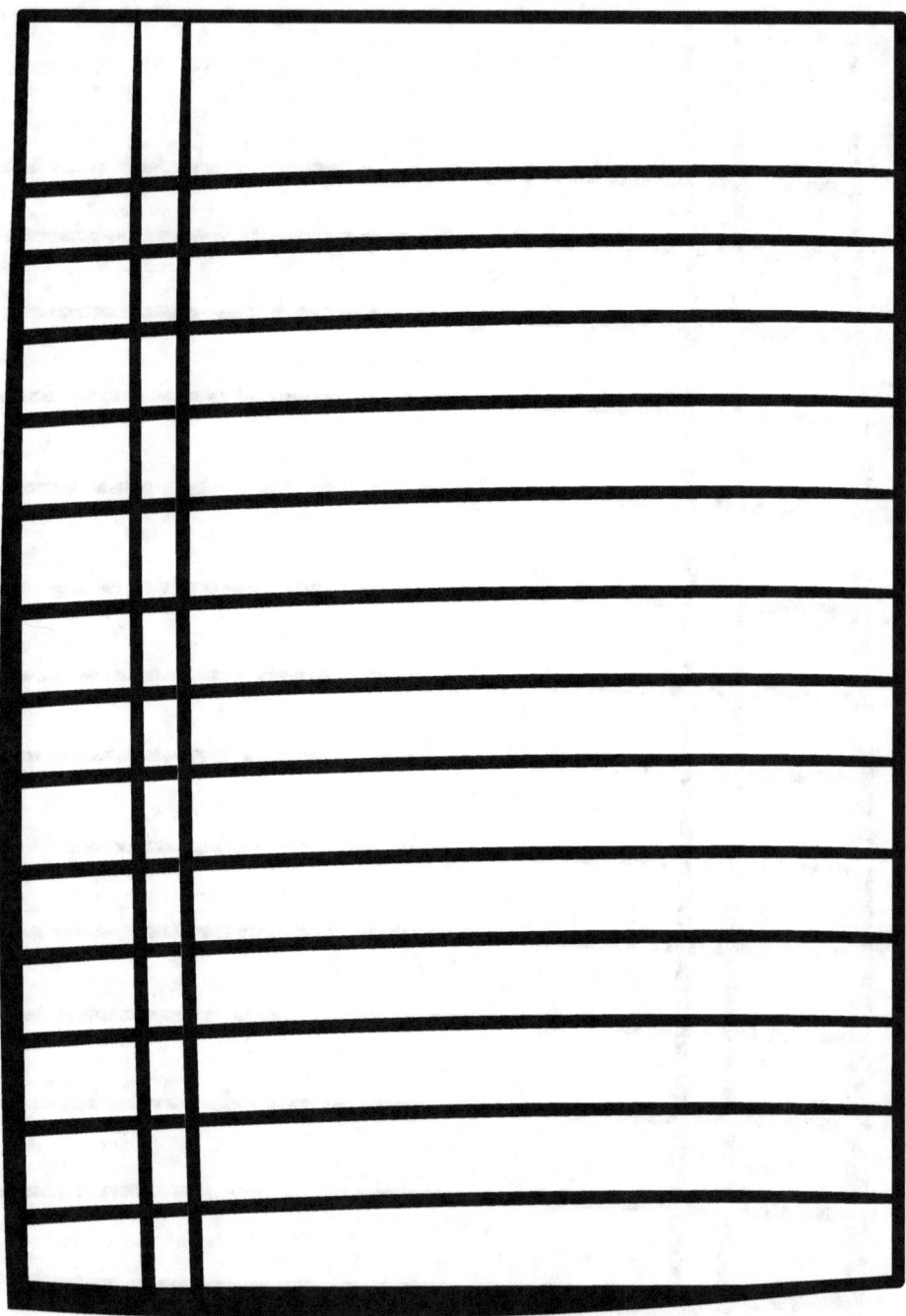

Books I am Reading

Book Title	Author

My favorite part of the book is:

_____
_____
_____
_____
_____
_____
_____
_____
_____
_____
_____
_____

Notes:

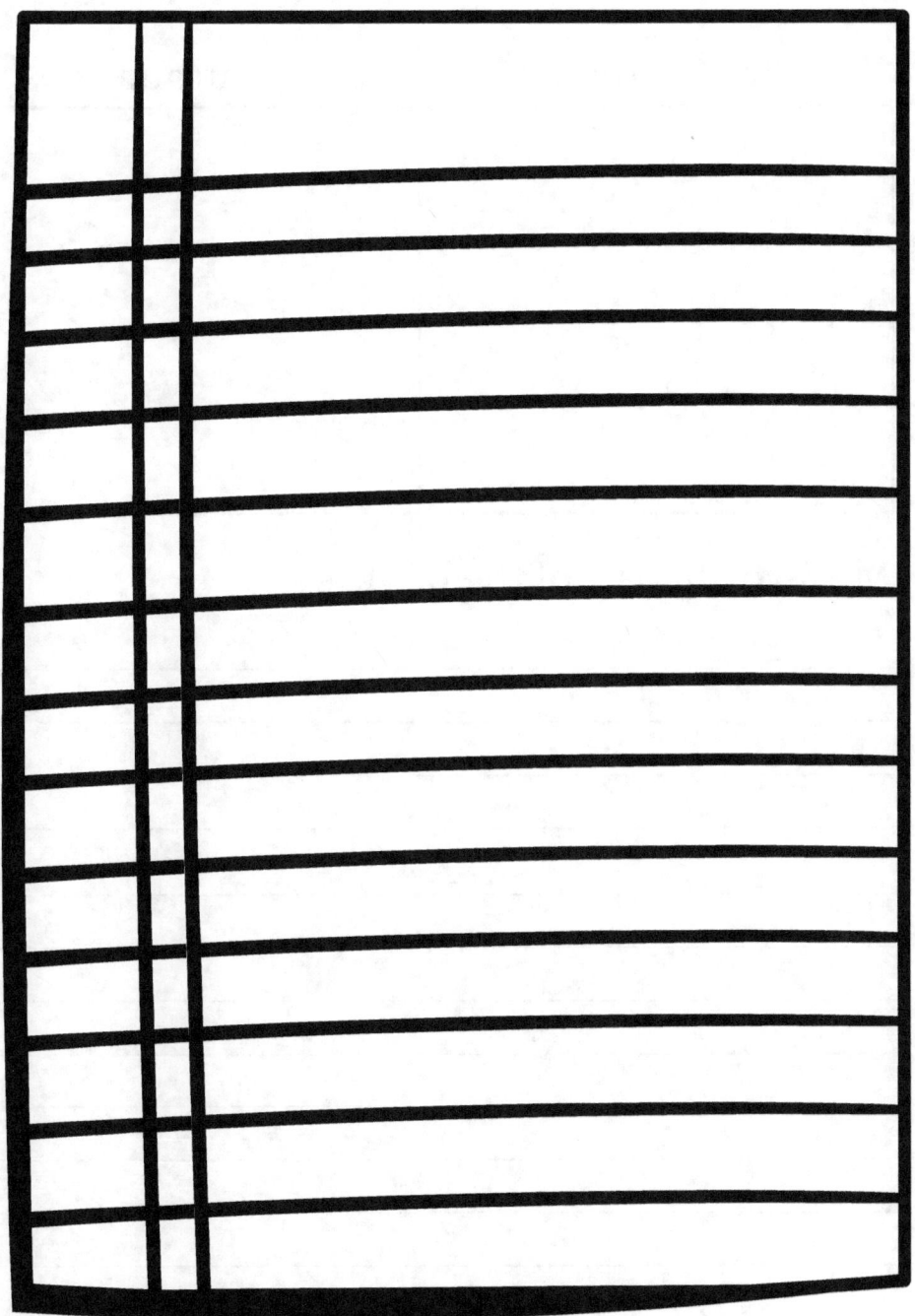

Books I am Reading

Book Title	Author

My favorite part of the book is:

_____
_____
_____
_____
_____
_____
_____
_____
_____
_____

Notes:

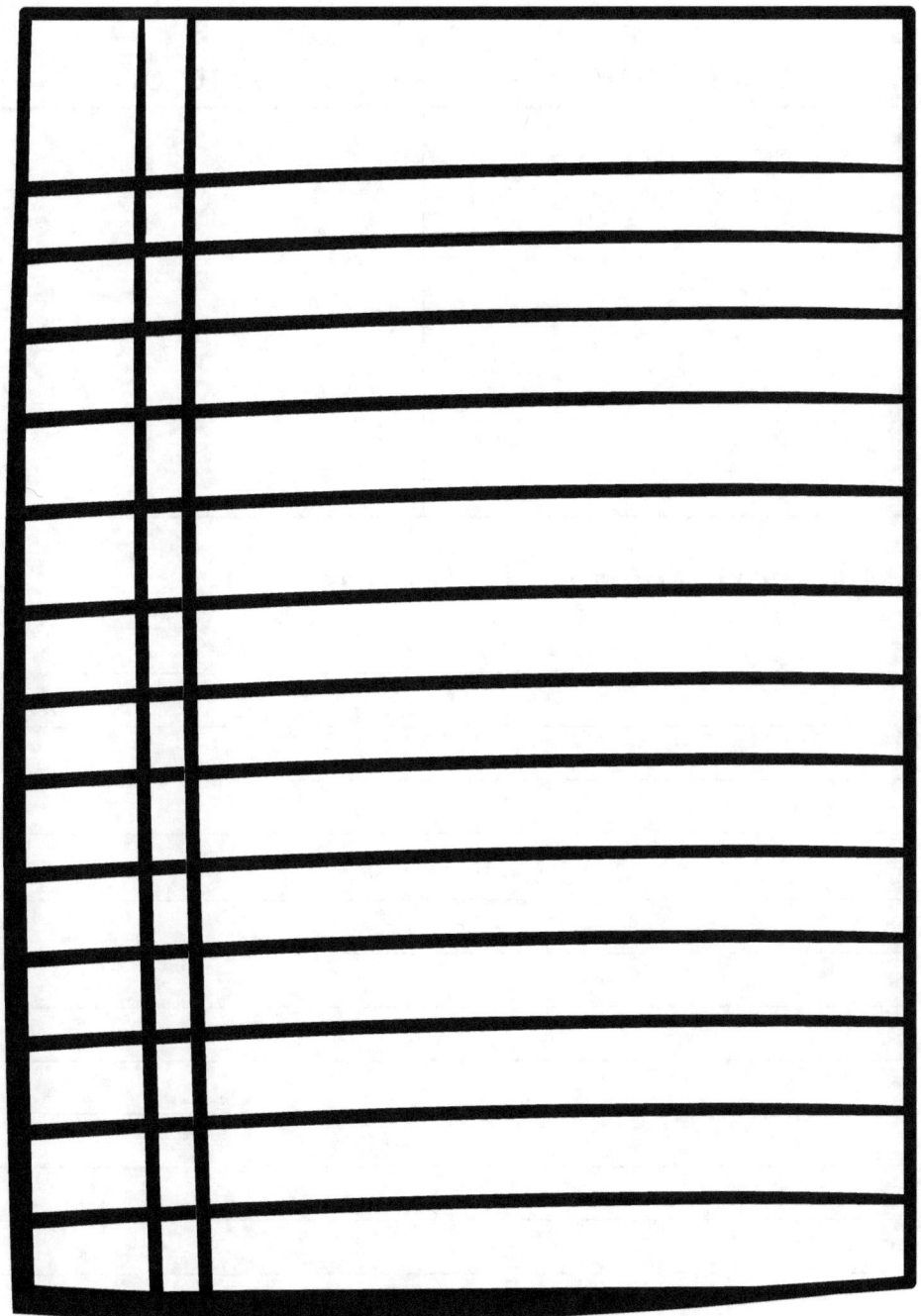

Books I am Reading

Book Title	Author

My favorite part of the book is:

_____
_____
_____
_____
_____
_____
_____
_____
_____
_____

Notes:

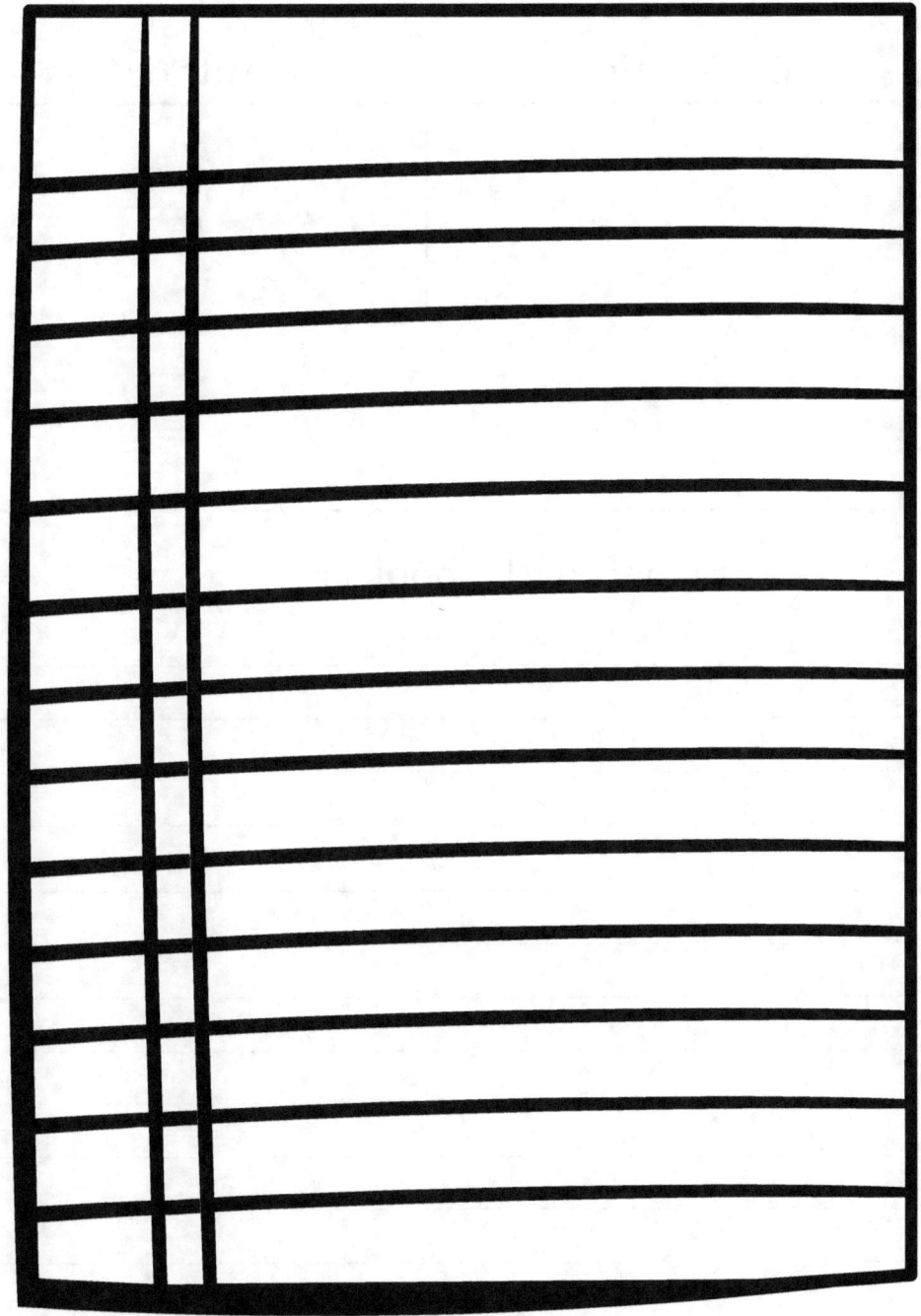

Books I am Reading

Book Title	Author

My favorite part of the book is:

_____
_____
_____
_____
_____
_____
_____
_____
_____
_____

Notes:

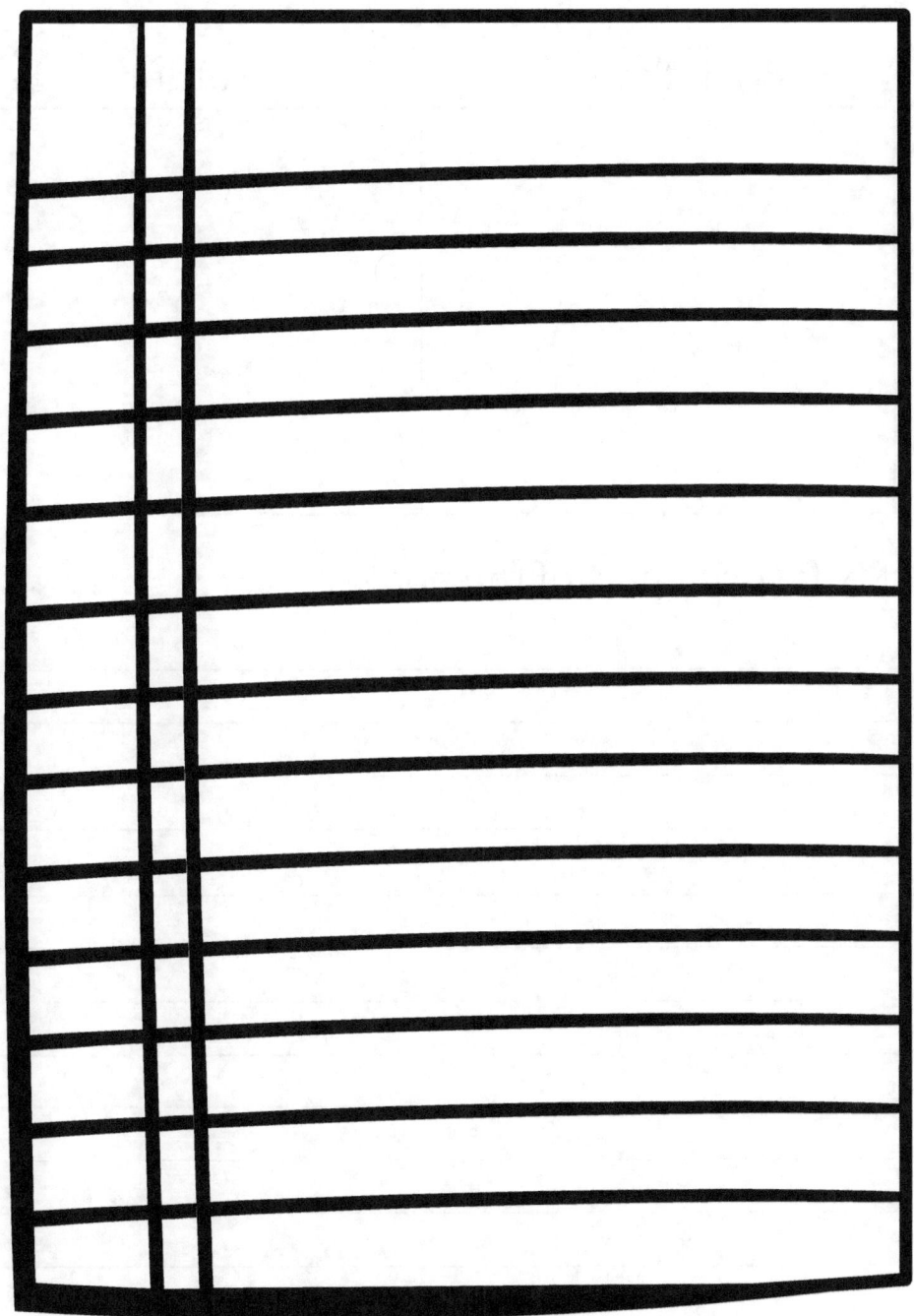

Books I am Reading

Book Title	Author

My favorite part of the book is:

_____
_____
_____
_____
_____
_____
_____
_____
_____
_____
_____

My Goal Think-Sheet

Things I would like to get better at:

_____
_____
_____
_____

I will be proud of myself if I accomplish this:

_____
_____
_____
_____

I would like to do this if I knew I couldn't fail:

_____
_____
_____
_____

My Goal Think-Sheet

Things I would like to get better at:

_____
_____
_____

I will be proud of myself if I accomplish this:

_____
_____
_____

I would like to do this if I knew I couldn't fail:

_____
_____
_____

Acts of Kindess

Things people did for me:

_____
_____
_____
_____
_____
_____
_____
_____

Things I did for other people:

_____
_____
_____
_____
_____
_____
_____
_____

Acts of Kindess

Things people did for me:

_____
_____
_____
_____
_____
_____
_____

Things I did for other people:

_____
_____
_____
_____
_____
_____
_____

Notes:

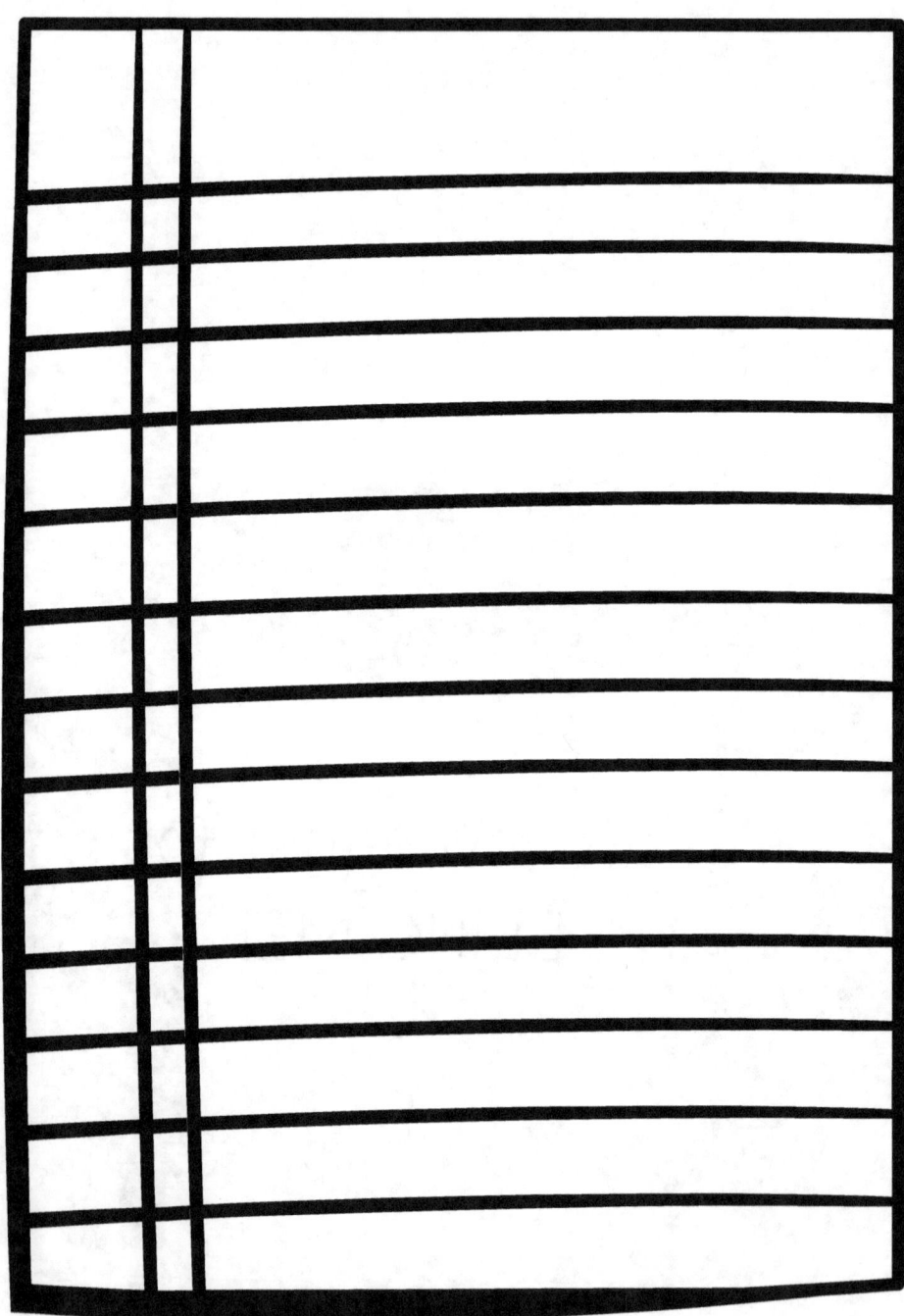

Notes:

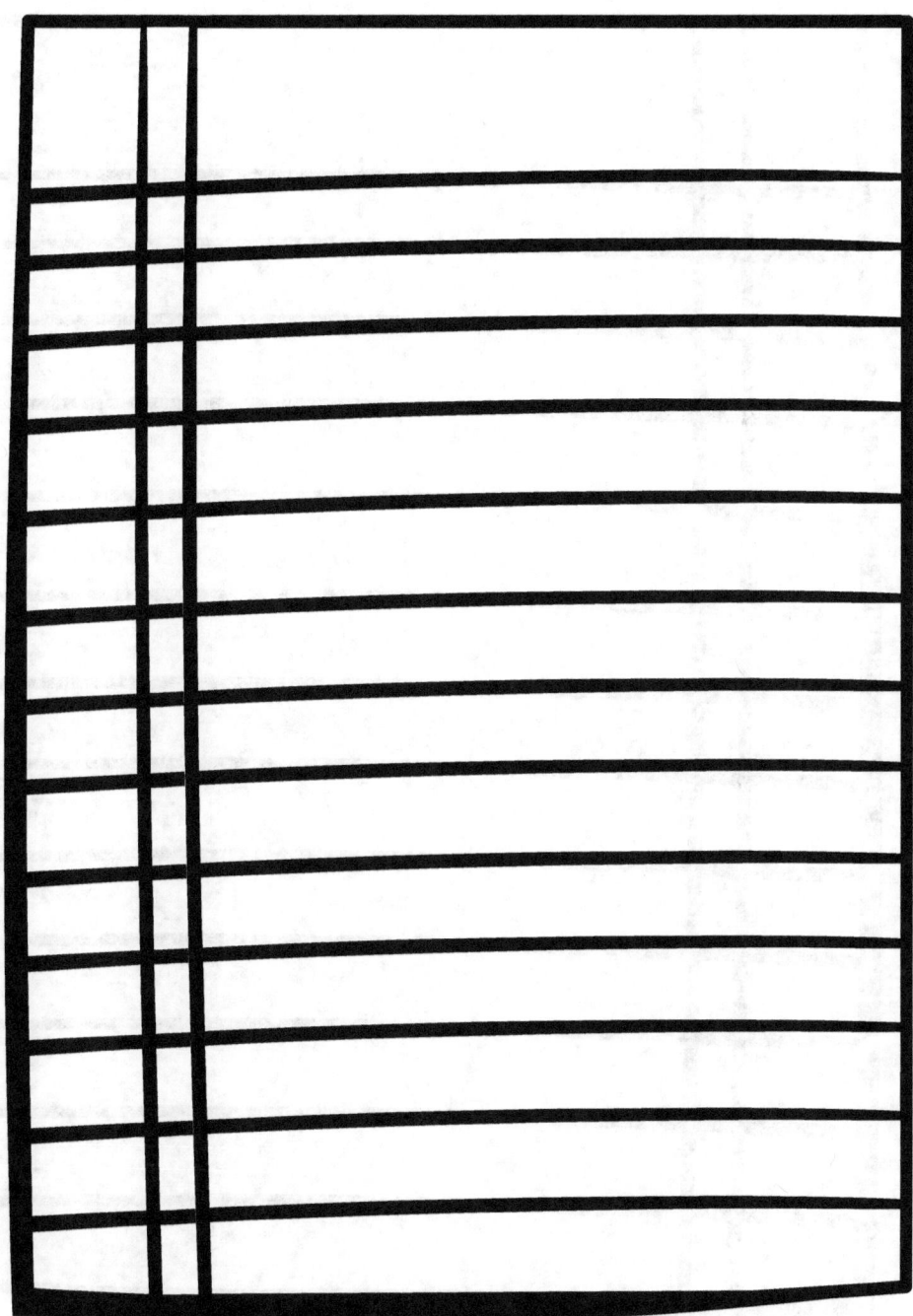

Notes:

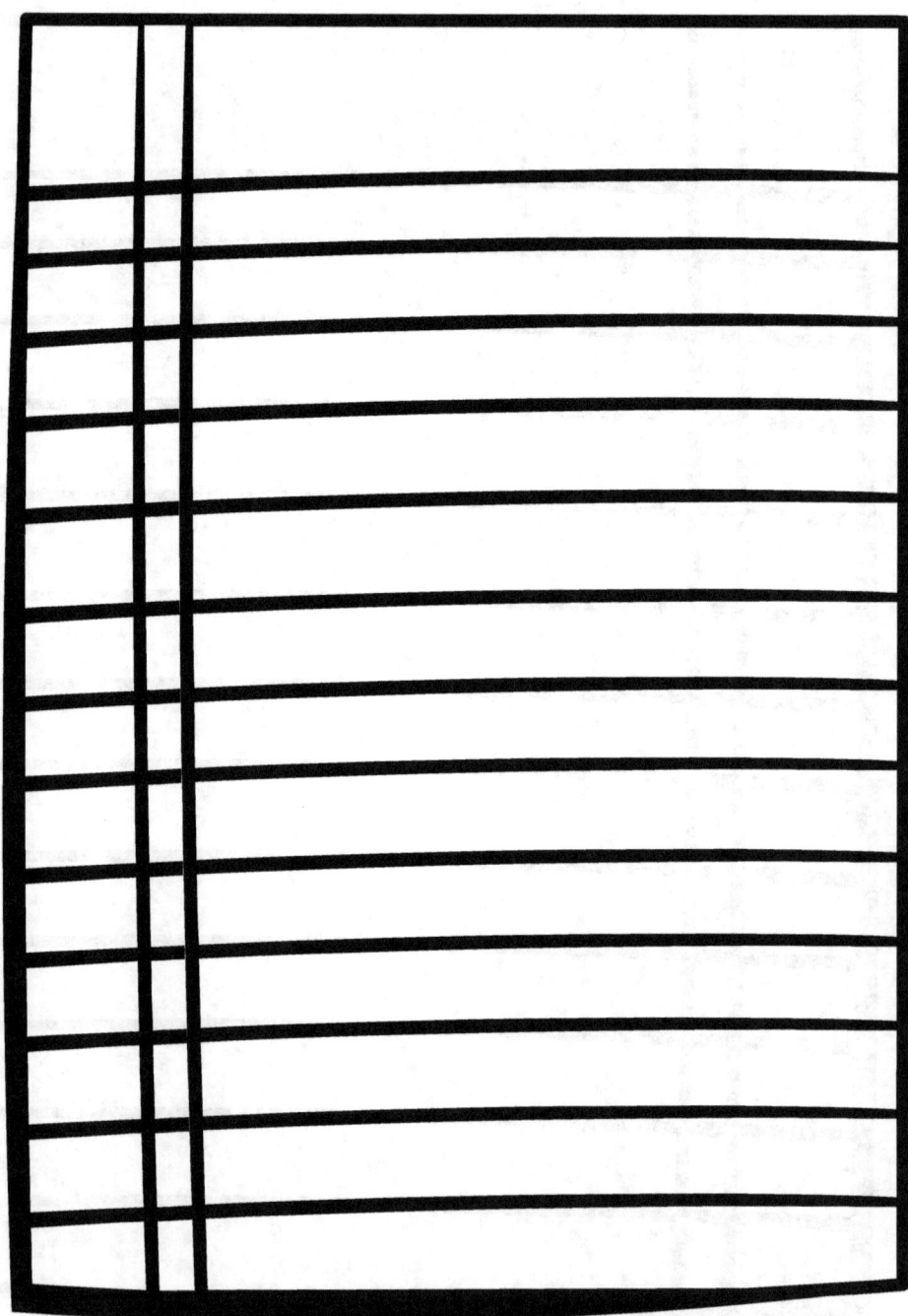

Notes:

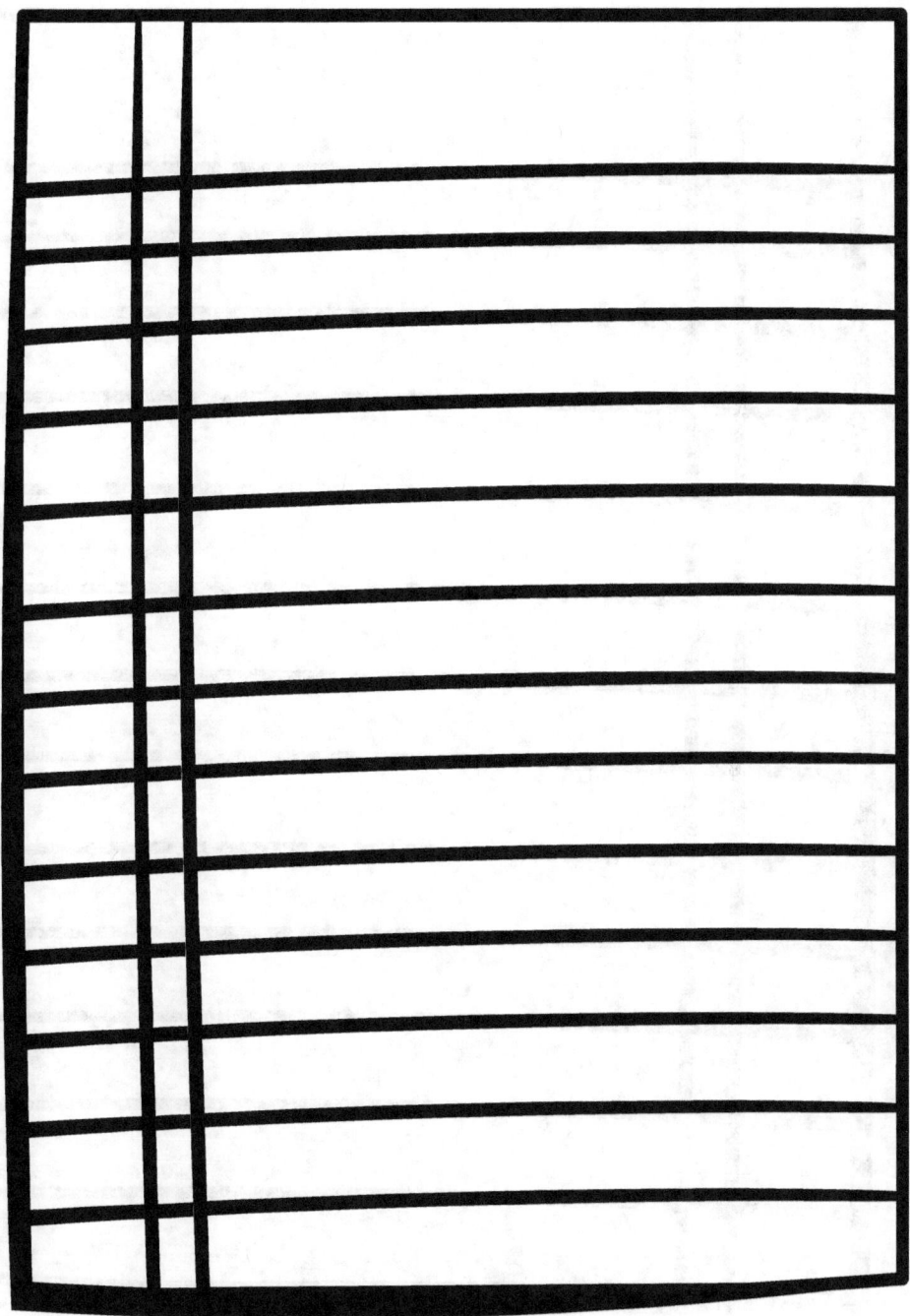

Notes:

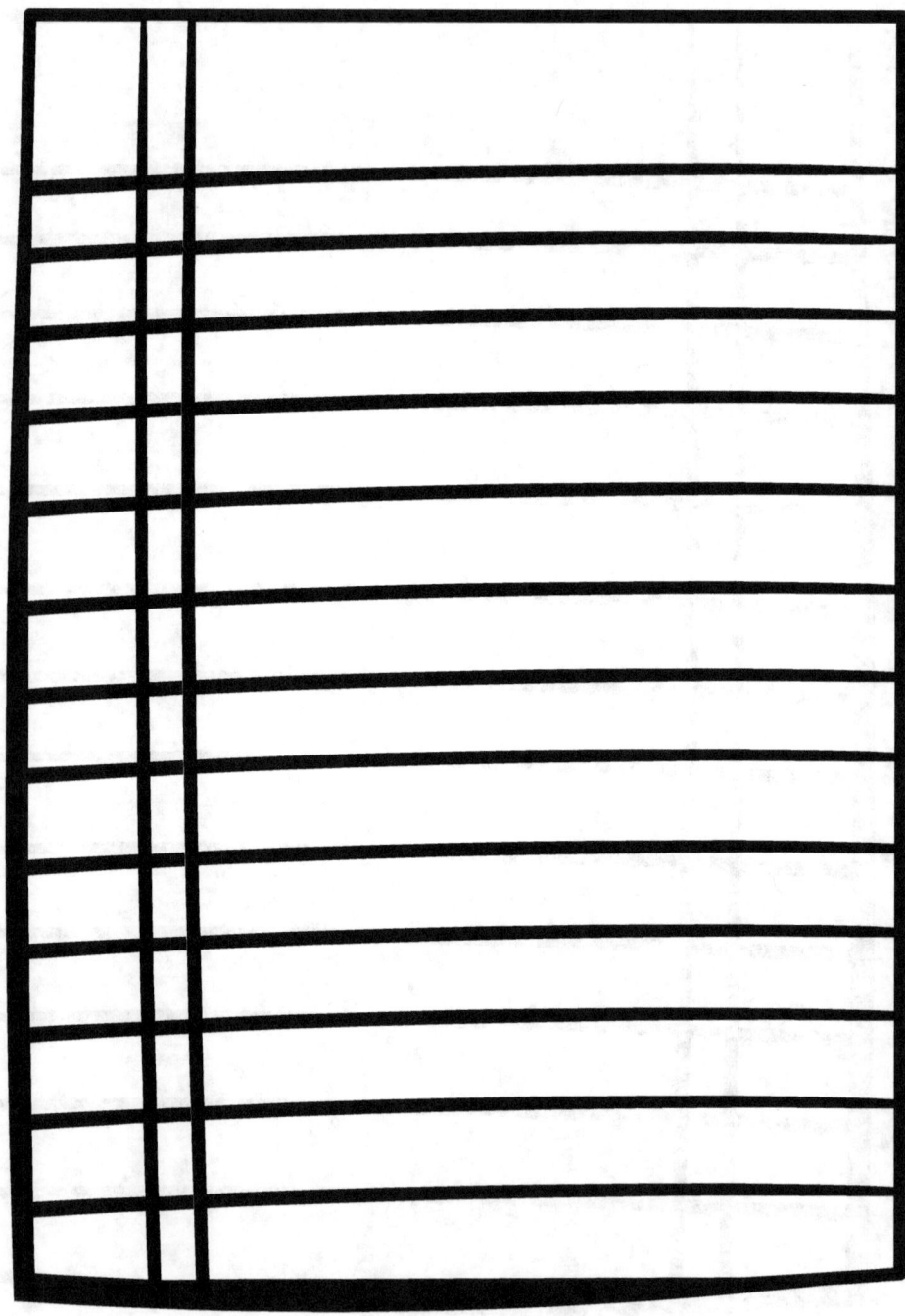

Notes:

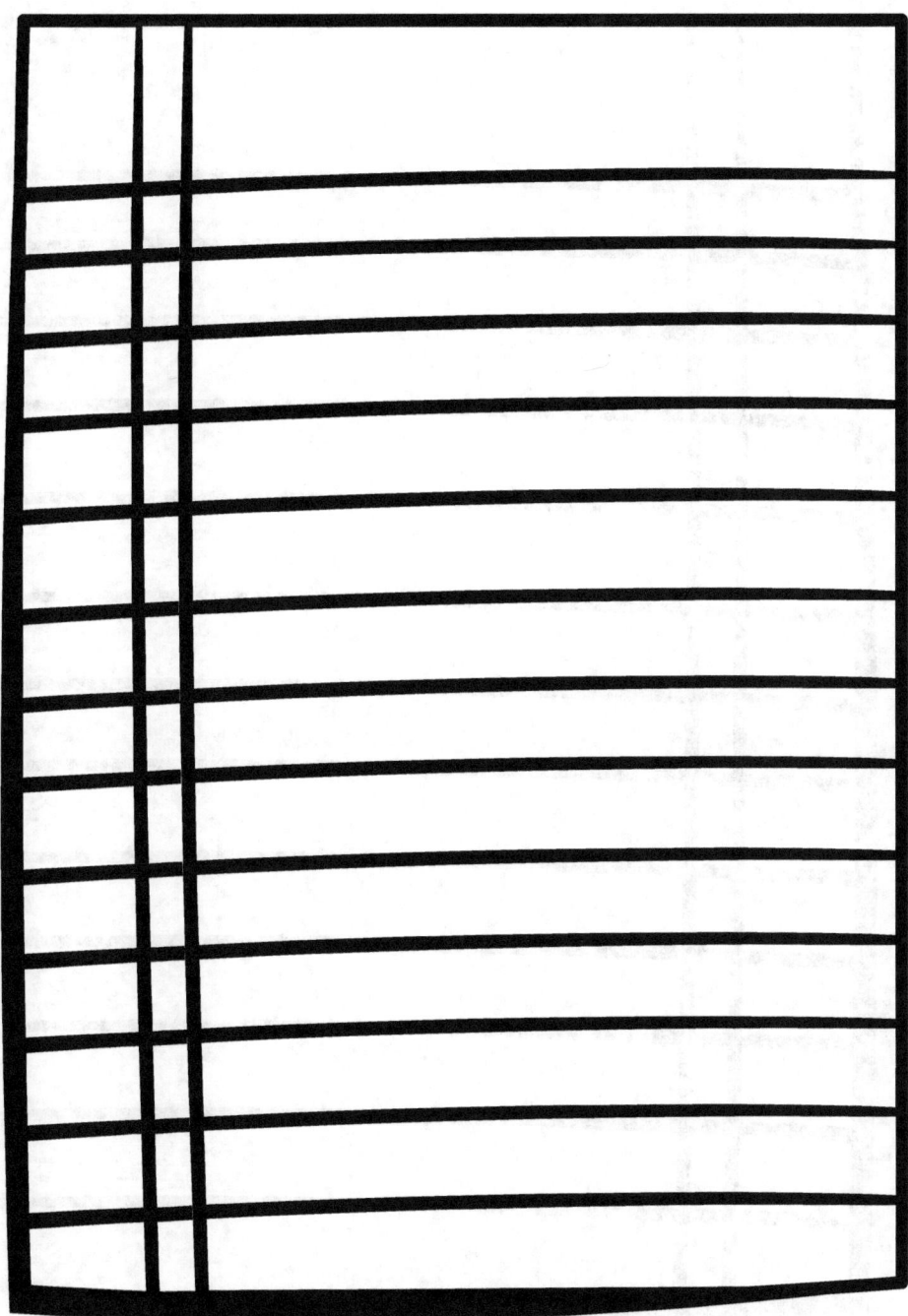

Notes:

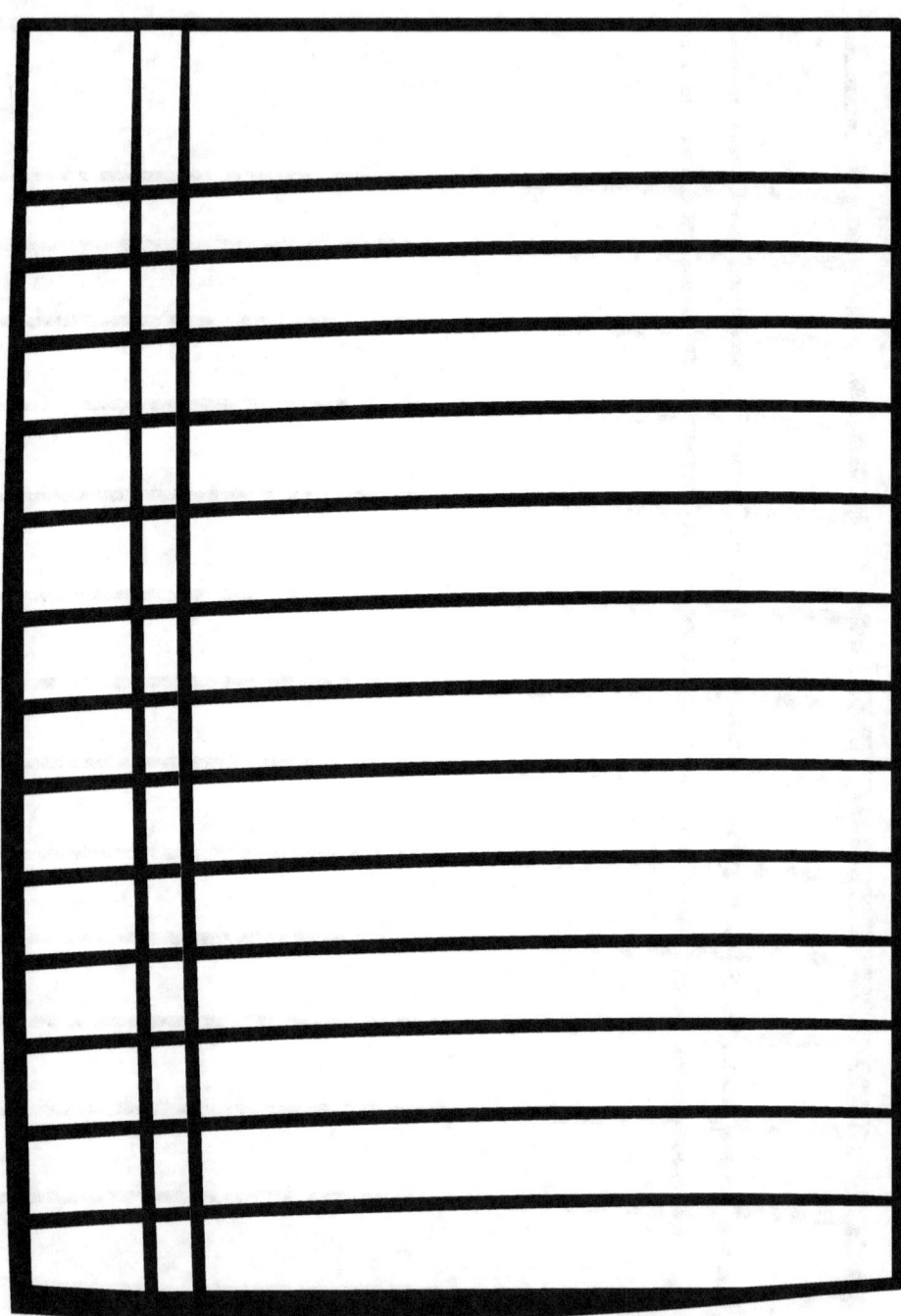

Notes:

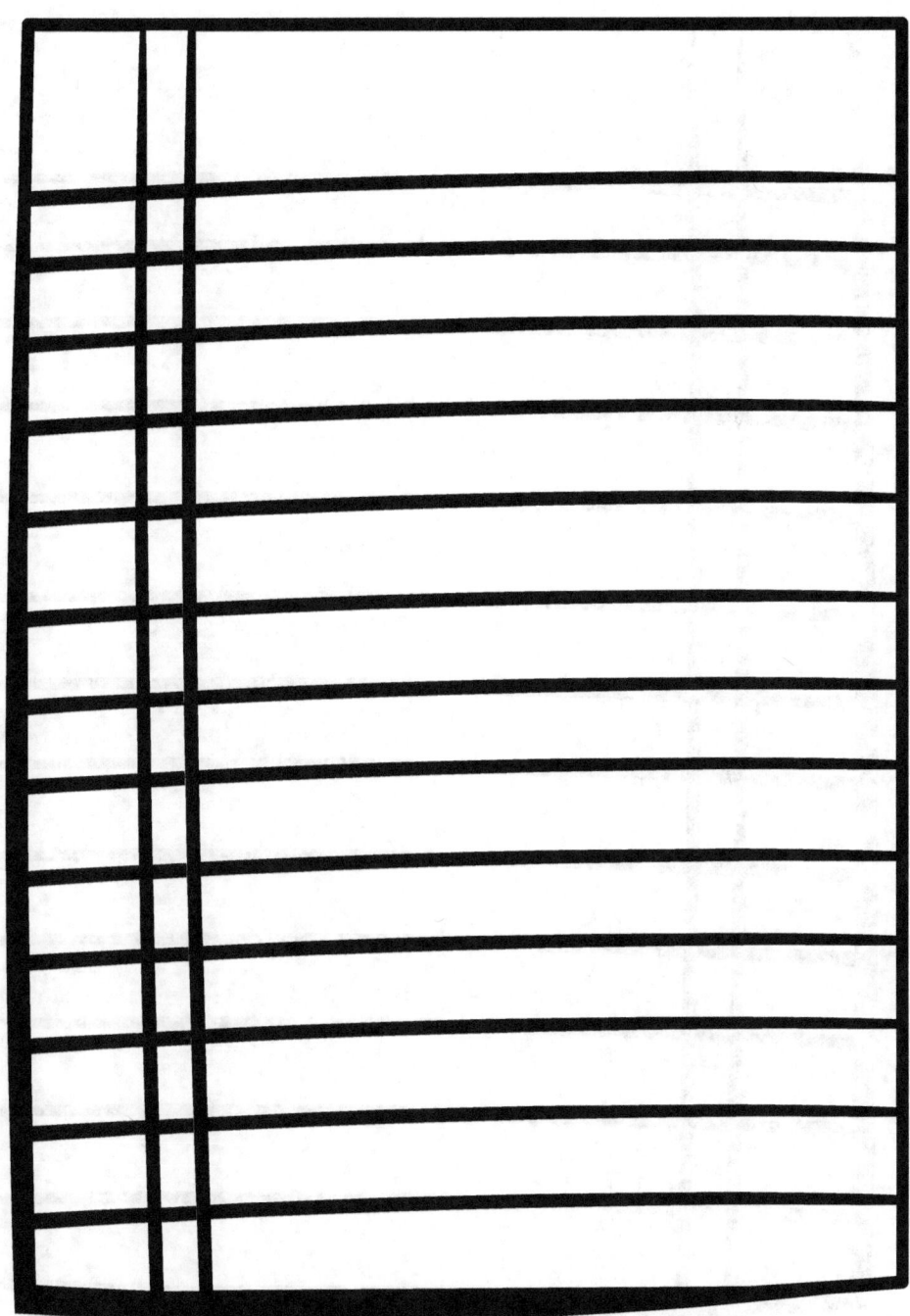

Notes:

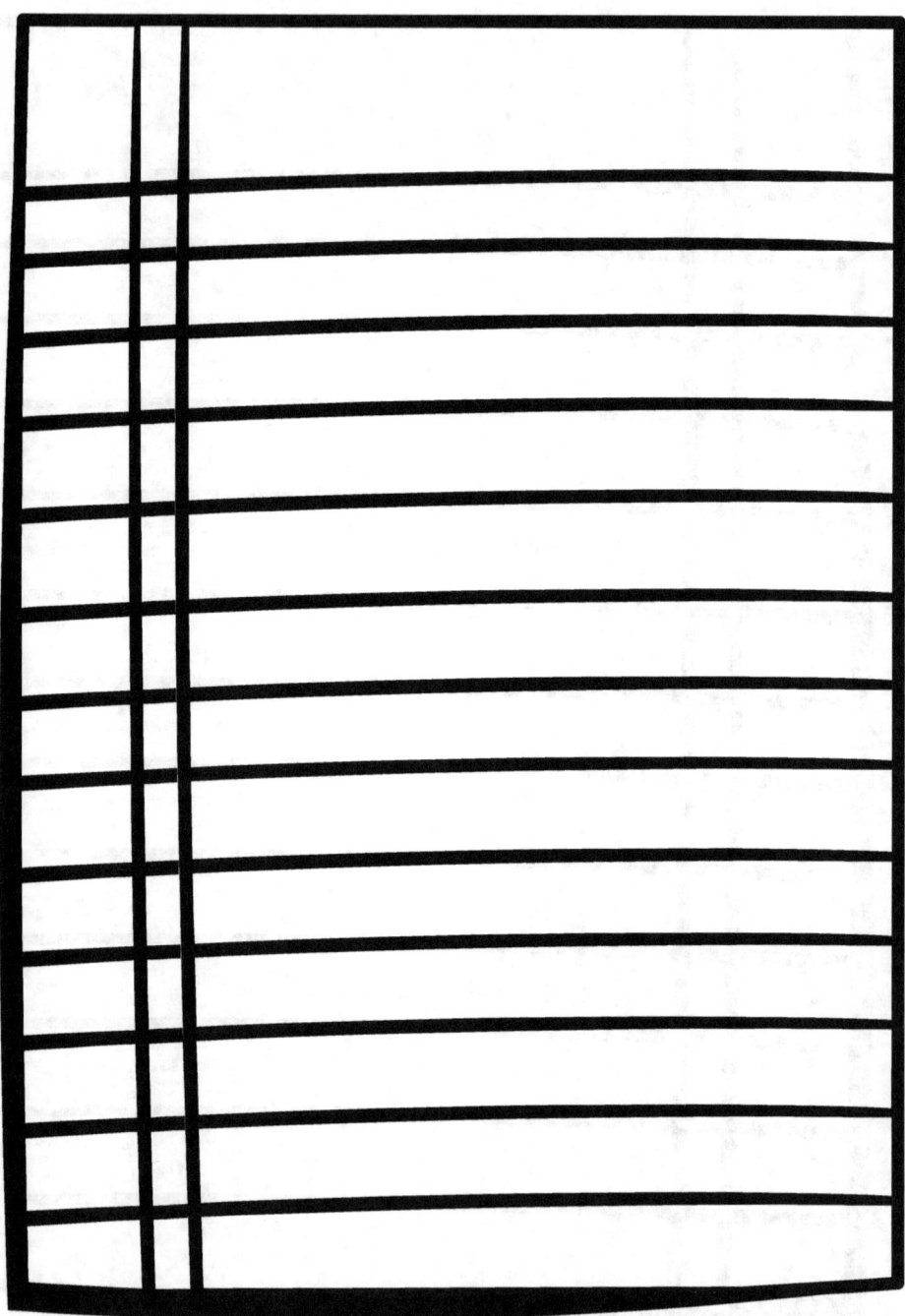

www.ingramcontent.com/pod-product-compliance
Lightning Source LLC
LaVergne TN
LVHW051956060526
838201LV00059B/3670